I0013149

Python AI for Beginners

Build Your First Machine Learning Project Today

THOMPSON CARTER

Table of Content

TABLE OF CONTENTS

INTRODUCTION

Python AI for Beginners: Build Your First Machine Learning Project Today"

Welcome to **"Python AI for Beginners: Build Your First Machine Learning Project Today"**—a hands-on guide designed to help you navigate the exciting world of artificial intelligence (AI) and machine learning (ML) with Python. Whether you are an absolute beginner or have some experience with programming, this book will guide you through every step of your learning journey in a clear, engaging, and practical way. Our goal is to empower you to understand the core concepts of AI and machine learning and equip you with the skills to build your own intelligent systems.

Why This Book?

In today's rapidly evolving world, AI and machine learning are at the forefront of technological advancements. From self-driving cars to personalized healthcare, AI is transforming industries, and the demand for skilled professionals in this field has never been greater. Python, with its simplicity and powerful libraries, has become the go-to language for AI and ML development, making it an ideal choice for this book.

This book is more than just a theoretical exploration of AI and machine learning. It's a **practical, hands-on guide** that takes you from understanding the basics to building your first machine learning project. We aim to demystify complex concepts and present them in an accessible manner, ensuring that you develop both theoretical knowledge and practical skills.

What Will You Learn?

Throughout this book, we will cover key topics in AI and machine learning, such as:

- **Introduction to Python and AI**: Understand what AI is, why Python is the ideal language for AI projects, and how to set up your development environment to start coding.
- **Basic Machine Learning Concepts**: Learn the foundational principles of machine learning, including supervised vs. unsupervised learning, data preprocessing, and the key algorithms that power AI systems.
- **Building Your First Machine Learning Model**: Step-by-step instructions on creating your first machine learning model using Python's powerful libraries, including **NumPy, Pandas, Matplotlib**, and **Scikit-learn**.
- **Deep Learning**: Dive into neural networks, including **Convolutional Neural Networks (CNNs)** and **Recurrent Neural Networks (RNNs)**, and learn how these models are used in real-world applications like image and speech recognition.

- **Natural Language Processing (NLP)**: Discover how AI systems understand and generate human language, and build a simple chatbot to interact with users.
- **Advanced Topics**: Explore topics like reinforcement learning, transfer learning, and AI ethics, providing a comprehensive view of the broader AI landscape.

Why AI and Machine Learning?

AI and machine learning have permeated nearly every aspect of modern life. Machine learning models can help businesses make data-driven decisions, improve customer experiences, and unlock new opportunities. They power applications like recommendation systems (e.g., Netflix and Amazon), virtual assistants (e.g., Siri and Alexa), fraud detection, medical diagnosis, and more.

Learning AI isn't just about the technology—it's about the ability to **solve real-world problems**. Whether you're aiming to work in data science, finance, healthcare, or software engineering, understanding AI and machine learning will open up countless opportunities for career growth, problem-solving, and innovation.

How This Book Will Help You

1. **Clear, Step-by-Step Approach**: This book takes a **gradual approach** to learning. Each chapter builds on the previous one, and each

concept is explained with clear, actionable instructions. By the end of the book, you will not only understand how to work with AI and machine learning models but also be able to implement them on your own.

2. **Real-World Projects**: You won't just learn theory; you'll apply it. Each chapter includes **hands-on projects** and exercises that allow you to put your knowledge to the test in real-world scenarios. You will build your own models, train them, and evaluate their performance.

3. **Beginner-Friendly**: No prior experience with AI or machine learning is necessary. We start with the basics, assuming only familiarity with programming in Python. Even if you've never worked with machine learning before, you'll be guided through the concepts, tools, and libraries in an approachable manner.

4. **Comprehensive yet Focused**: We cover everything from **basic machine learning models** to **deep learning** and **natural language processing**, ensuring you gain a broad understanding of the field. However, the focus is on building practical skills—so you can implement what you've learned in projects.

5. **Real-World Applications**: AI is most impactful when it is used to solve real problems. This book explores practical use cases such as predicting customer behavior, building recommendation systems, and creating chatbots, all of which are highly relevant to the needs of the modern tech industry.

Who Is This Book For?

This book is designed for anyone who wants to get started with AI and machine learning, regardless of their background. If you are:

- A **beginner** with no prior experience in machine learning or AI, this book will give you the foundation to build a solid understanding.
- A **programmer** looking to expand your skill set into the realm of AI and machine learning, this book will introduce you to Python's AI ecosystem and provide the hands-on experience needed to build models.
- A **data enthusiast** interested in applying AI to real-world problems, this book will guide you in developing practical AI models for different applications.

What You'll Need

To follow along with this book, you will need:

- A **basic understanding of Python** programming. We assume you know how to write Python code, work with variables, and use control structures like loops and conditionals.
- A **working Python environment**: You will need Python installed on your computer, along with libraries like **NumPy**, **Pandas**, **Matplotlib**, and **Scikit-learn** (which we'll help you install).

- **Jupyter Notebooks** or another Python IDE (like **PyCharm** or **VS Code**) to run your code and visualize results.

What to Expect from Each Chapter

Each chapter is structured to maximize learning:

- **Introduction**: A brief overview of the chapter's content and objectives.
- **Theory**: We'll explain the key concepts and techniques you'll be using in simple terms.
- **Hands-On Projects**: Each chapter includes coding examples, exercises, and a project that allows you to practice what you've learned.
- **Real-World Applications**: We emphasize how to apply machine learning techniques to real problems across various domains, such as healthcare, retail, and finance.
- **Conclusion**: A summary of the CHAPTER SUMMARY from the chapter and next steps to continue learning.

Your Next Steps

By the end of this book, you'll have the knowledge and confidence to:

- Build your own machine learning models using Python.
- Apply transfer learning to solve complex tasks.
- Understand the key challenges in AI, including bias and fairness.

- Stay up-to-date with the latest developments in AI and machine learning.

You'll also be ready to embark on **your own AI projects**, whether it's working on personal projects, contributing to open-source AI tools, or pursuing a career in AI. This book serves as a stepping stone to a fulfilling journey in one of the most exciting and rapidly growing fields in technology.

So, let's dive in! Get ready to unlock the power of AI and machine learning and start building your first intelligent systems today!

CHAPTER 1

Introduction to AI and Python

Overview of AI: What is Artificial Intelligence?

Artificial Intelligence (AI) refers to the simulation of human intelligence in machines that are programmed to think, learn, and perform tasks typically requiring human intelligence. It involves creating algorithms that allow computers to process information, make decisions, recognize patterns, and improve over time through learning.

AI can be broadly categorized into:

- **Narrow AI**: AI designed to perform a specific task, such as facial recognition or voice assistants like Siri.
- **General AI**: A more advanced, theoretical form of AI that can perform any intellectual task that a human can do. It is still under research and development.

Importance of Python in AI and Why It's the Go-To Language for Machine Learning

Python is the most popular programming language for AI and machine learning due to several key reasons:

1. **Ease of Use**: Python's simple and readable syntax makes it easy to learn and use, even for beginners.

14

2. **Extensive Libraries**: Python has a rich ecosystem of libraries for AI and machine learning, such as:
   - **TensorFlow** and **Keras** for deep learning.
   - **Scikit-learn** for traditional machine learning algorithms.
   - **NumPy** and **Pandas** for data manipulation and analysis.
3. **Community Support**: Python has a large, active community that continually contributes to its growth and offers support through forums, tutorials, and open-source projects.
4. **Integration**: Python integrates well with other languages and platforms, allowing you to build complex AI systems with ease.

Installing Python and Setting Up Your Development Environment

To get started with Python for AI development, follow these steps:

1. **Install Python**:
   - Go to the official Python website: python.org.
   - Download the latest version of Python (3.x) for your operating system (Windows, macOS, or Linux).
   - Follow the installation instructions for your platform.
2. **Install a Code Editor/IDE**:

- o **VS Code** or **PyCharm** are popular editors for Python development.
- o You can also use Jupyter Notebooks, which we'll discuss next.

3. **Setting up Python Environment with pip**:
   - o Open the terminal (or command prompt) and type:

```bash

python --version
```

This should display the version of Python installed.

   - o Install **pip**, the Python package manager, if not already installed:

```bash

python -m ensurepip --upgrade
```

4. **Install Necessary Libraries**: Use **pip** to install essential libraries for machine learning:

```bash

pip install numpy pandas matplotlib scikit-learn tensorflow
```

Introduction to Jupyter Notebooks for Interactive Coding

Jupyter Notebooks are an interactive web-based environment that allows you to write and execute Python code in cells. It's an essential tool for data science, machine learning, and AI development. You can combine code, visualizations, and narrative in a single document, which makes it ideal for experimenting and documenting your AI projects.

To set up Jupyter Notebooks:

1. Install Jupyter using pip:

   ```bash
   pip install notebook
   ```

2. Start the Jupyter Notebook server:

   ```bash
   jupyter notebook
   ```

3. This will open the Jupyter interface in your web browser, where you can create new notebooks and start coding.

A Simple "Hello World" Python Program to Kickstart Your Journey

Let's start with a simple Python program to make sure everything is set up correctly:

1. Open your Python editor or Jupyter Notebook.
2. In the editor or a new Jupyter Notebook cell, write the following code:

```python
# Simple "Hello World" program
print("Hello, World!")
```

3. Run the program, and you should see the output:

```
Hello, World!
```

This is your first Python program, and it's the foundation for every project you'll build in AI. Python's simplicity makes it an excellent starting point for your journey into machine learning and AI development.

This chapter sets the stage for understanding AI and Python, providing the essential setup steps and your first interaction with Python code. Ready to move on to Chapter 2 or need any changes?

CHAPTER 2

Understanding the Foundations of Machine Learning

What is Machine Learning?

Machine Learning (ML) is a subset of Artificial Intelligence (AI) that enables computers to learn from data without being explicitly programmed. Instead of following rigid instructions, ML algorithms use patterns and statistical techniques to improve their performance over time as they process more data.

In essence, ML allows a system to automatically improve itself based on experience. The process involves feeding data into an algorithm, training the algorithm to recognize patterns, and making predictions or decisions based on new, unseen data.

Supervised vs. Unsupervised Learning: Key Differences

Machine Learning is typically categorized into two main types: **Supervised Learning** and **Unsupervised Learning**.

1. **Supervised Learning**:
   o In supervised learning, the algorithm is trained on a labeled dataset, where both the input data and the corresponding correct output (target) are provided.

o The goal is to learn a mapping from inputs to outputs to make predictions for new, unseen data.
o **Examples**:
   ▪ Predicting house prices based on features like size, location, etc.
   ▪ Classifying emails as spam or not spam.

Real-world example: A supervised learning task could be predicting the amount of rainfall based on historical weather data.

2. **Unsupervised Learning**:
   o Unsupervised learning, on the other hand, deals with unlabeled data. The algorithm must find hidden patterns or intrinsic structures in the data without pre-defined labels.
   o The goal is often to group similar data points together (clustering) or reduce the dimensionality of data (dimensionality reduction).
   o **Examples**:
      ▪ Customer segmentation based on purchasing behavior.
      ▪ Grouping news articles based on topics without predefined categories.

Real-world example: An e-commerce company might use unsupervised learning to cluster customers into segments based on their browsing and buying habits.

The Role of Data in Machine Learning

Data is at the heart of every machine learning algorithm. The quality and quantity of data directly impact the performance of machine learning models. The more relevant and varied the data, the better the model can generalize and make accurate predictions.

Key aspects of data in ML:

- **Training Data**: The data used to train the model, typically a large dataset that includes both input features and target labels (in supervised learning).
- **Testing Data**: The data used to evaluate the model's performance after training. This data helps assess how well the model generalizes to unseen data.
- **Feature Engineering**: The process of selecting, transforming, or creating new features from raw data to improve the model's performance.

How Machine Learning Models Learn from Data

Machine learning models learn through the process of training, where they adjust their parameters to minimize the error between the model's predictions and the actual target values. This process involves:

1. **Feeding the Model**: The model is presented with input data.
2. **Making Predictions**: The model makes predictions based on its current parameters.
3. **Calculating the Error**: The difference between the predicted and actual values is calculated using a loss function.
4. **Updating the Model**: Using algorithms like gradient descent, the model adjusts its parameters to reduce this error. This process repeats until the model reaches an optimal set of parameters.

This learning process continues as the model is trained on more data, and it becomes increasingly accurate over time.

Overview of Common Machine Learning Algorithms

Machine learning algorithms can be broadly classified into several categories, each suited to different types of problems:

1. **Linear Regression**:
   - A simple algorithm used for predicting continuous outcomes (regression tasks). It tries to fit a straight line that best represents the relationship between the input features and the output.
   - **Example**: Predicting house prices based on features like square footage, number of bedrooms, etc.
2. **Logistic Regression**:

- o Used for binary classification tasks. Despite its name, logistic regression is a classification algorithm, not a regression algorithm.
- o **Example**: Predicting whether a customer will buy a product (Yes/No) based on their browsing behavior.

3. **Decision Trees**:
- o A tree-like model that splits data into subsets based on the most significant feature at each node. It's easy to interpret and visualize.
- o **Example**: Classifying animals based on features like size, habitat, and diet.

4. **Support Vector Machines (SVM)**:
- o A classification algorithm that finds the optimal hyperplane to separate data points into different classes.
- o **Example**: Classifying emails as spam or not spam.

5. **K-Nearest Neighbors (KNN)**:
- o A simple classification algorithm that assigns a data point to the most common class among its K nearest neighbors.
- o **Example**: Identifying the genre of a book based on its characteristics (e.g., number of pages, author, publication date).

6. **K-Means Clustering**:
- o An unsupervised algorithm used for grouping similar data points into clusters. It's widely used for clustering problems.

o **Example**: Grouping customers into different market segments based on their purchasing behavior.

Real-world Example: Predicting House Prices Using Linear Regression

Let's apply the concept of supervised learning and linear regression to predict house prices based on input features such as square footage, number of bedrooms, and location.

Step-by-step example:

1. **Import the necessary libraries**:

python

```
import numpy as np
import pandas as pd
from sklearn.model_selection import
train_test_split
from sklearn.linear_model import
LinearRegression
from sklearn.metrics import
mean_squared_error
import matplotlib.pyplot as plt
```

2. **Load the dataset**: For simplicity, we'll assume you have a CSV file with house prices and features like `Square_Feet`, `Bedrooms`, and `Location`.

```python
python

# Load dataset
data                                =
pd.read_csv("house_prices.csv")
print(data.head())
```

3. **Prepare the data**: Split the data into input features (X) and the target variable (y).

```python
python

X = data[['Square_Feet', 'Bedrooms',
'Location']]
y = data['Price']
```

4. **Split the data into training and testing sets**:

```python
python

X_train, X_test, y_train, y_test =
train_test_split(X, y, test_size=0.2,
random_state=42)
```

5. **Train the linear regression model**:

```python
python

model = LinearRegression()
model.fit(X_train, y_train)
```

6. **Make predictions**:

```python
python
```

```
y_pred = model.predict(X_test)
```

7. Evaluate the model:

python

```
mse = mean_squared_error(y_test, y_pred)
print(f"Mean Squared Error: {mse}")
```

8. Visualize the results:

python

```
plt.scatter(y_test, y_pred)
plt.xlabel("True Prices")
plt.ylabel("Predicted Prices")
plt.title("House Price Prediction")
plt.show()
```

In this example, you train a simple linear regression model to predict house prices based on features. The mean squared error (MSE) gives you a sense of how well your model is performing.

This chapter gives you a solid understanding of the fundamentals of machine learning, including key algorithms, data preparation, and a hands-on example with linear regression. Ready to proceed with the next chapter,

CHAPTER 3

Setting Up Your First Python Project for Machine Learning

How to Create a Machine Learning Project in Python

When starting a machine learning project, it's important to structure your codebase in a way that makes it easy to work with, manage, and scale. Here's a simple approach to creating a well-organized machine learning project:

1. **Create a Project Directory**:
   - Create a new directory for your project to keep everything organized.
   - Example:

   ```bash
   ```

   ```bash
   mkdir my_ml_project
   cd my_ml_project
   ```

2. **Create Virtual Environment**:
   - Using a virtual environment ensures that your project dependencies don't interfere with other projects.
   - To create and activate a virtual environment:

   ```bash
   ```

   ```bash
   python -m venv venv
   ```

```
source venv/bin/activate    #
On macOS/Linux
venv\Scripts\activate       #
On Windows
```

3. **Install Required Libraries**:
   o Use **pip** to install the necessary libraries for machine learning and data manipulation. At a minimum, you'll need:

```bash
```

```
pip install numpy pandas
matplotlib scikit-learn
```

4. **Project Structure**:
   o Organize your project into different folders for clarity. A common structure might look like this:

```bash
```

```
my_ml_project/
├── data/            # Store
datasets here
├── notebooks/       # Jupyter
notebooks              for
experimentation
├── scripts/         # Python
scripts for model building
and training
├── models/          # Trained
machine learning models
```

```
└── README.md          # Project
documentation
```

5. **Create a Jupyter Notebook or Python Script**:
   - You can start coding in Jupyter Notebooks for experimentation or create a `.py` script for a more formal, production-ready project.

Overview of Libraries: NumPy, Pandas, Matplotlib, and Scikit-learn

Here's an overview of the most commonly used libraries for machine learning in Python:

1. **NumPy**:
   - NumPy is a powerful library for numerical computing in Python. It provides support for multi-dimensional arrays and matrices, along with a collection of mathematical functions to operate on them.
   - Key Features:
     - Efficient handling of large data arrays and matrices.
     - Mathematical operations like linear algebra, Fourier transforms, and random number generation.
     - Used extensively in ML for data manipulation and feature extraction.
2. **Pandas**:

- o Pandas is an open-source library that provides easy-to-use data structures and data analysis tools. It is built on top of NumPy and provides data structures like `DataFrame` and `Series` for handling structured data (e.g., CSVs, SQL databases).
- o Key Features:
  - Efficient handling of labeled, multidimensional data.
  - Functions for data cleaning, merging, reshaping, and analysis.

3. **Matplotlib**:
   - o Matplotlib is a data visualization library that allows you to create static, animated, and interactive plots. It is commonly used to visualize machine learning data and results.
   - o Key Features:
     - Provides a wide variety of plot types (line, bar, scatter, histogram, etc.).
     - Customizable charts for publication-quality visuals.

4. **Scikit-learn**:
   - o Scikit-learn is one of the most widely used libraries for machine learning in Python. It provides simple and efficient tools for data mining and data analysis.
   - o Key Features:
     - Algorithms for classification, regression, clustering, and dimensionality reduction.

- Tools for model evaluation and validation (e.g., cross-validation, metrics).
- Extensive documentation and community support.

Loading and Handling Datasets in Python

Before you can train machine learning models, you need to load and handle your datasets. Let's take a look at how to load and manipulate datasets using **Pandas** and **NumPy**:

1. **Loading Data**: You can load datasets from a variety of formats (CSV, Excel, JSON, SQL, etc.). For this example, we'll load a CSV file containing data.

```python
import pandas as pd

# Load a dataset from a CSV file
data                              =
pd.read_csv('path/to/dataset.csv')

# Display the first 5 rows of the
dataset
print(data.head())
```

2. **Handling Missing Data**: Often, real-world datasets have missing or incomplete data. You

can handle missing values by either filling them with the mean/median or dropping them.

python

```
# Fill missing values with the mean of
each column
data.fillna(data.mean(),
inplace=True)

# Drop rows with missing values
data.dropna(inplace=True)
```

3. **Selecting Features and Target Variables**: Once you've cleaned your data, you can separate the features (input variables) from the target variable (the variable you're trying to predict).

python

```
# Selecting features (X) and target
(y)
X = data[['Feature1', 'Feature2',
'Feature3']]  # Replace with actual
feature names
y = data['Target']  # Replace with the
actual target column name
```

Visualizing Data with Matplotlib

Data visualization is a crucial step in understanding the underlying patterns and distributions in your dataset. **Matplotlib** is the go-to library for plotting.

1. **Plotting a Simple Line Plot**: A line plot can be used to show the relationship between two variables.

```python
import matplotlib.pyplot as plt

# Plotting a simple line graph
plt.plot(data['Feature1'],
data['Target'])
plt.xlabel('Feature1')
plt.ylabel('Target')
plt.title('Feature1 vs Target')
plt.show()
```

2. **Plotting a Histogram**: A histogram is useful for visualizing the distribution of a single variable.

```python
# Plotting a histogram of the target variable
plt.hist(data['Target'],    bins=10,
color='skyblue', edgecolor='black')
plt.xlabel('Target')
plt.ylabel('Frequency')
plt.title('Distribution of Target')
plt.show()
```

3. **Scatter Plot**: A scatter plot is great for visualizing the relationship between two numerical features.

```python

# Scatter plot to show relationship
between two features
plt.scatter(data['Feature1'],
data['Feature2'],          c='blue',
alpha=0.5)
plt.xlabel('Feature1')
plt.ylabel('Feature2')
plt.title('Feature1 vs Feature2')
plt.show()
```

Hands-on Example: Data Visualization and Basic Statistics

Let's now put everything together with a hands-on example using **Pandas** and **Matplotlib**.

1. **Load a sample dataset** (e.g., the famous Iris dataset):

```python

from   sklearn.datasets   import
load_iris

# Load the Iris dataset
iris = load_iris()
data   =   pd.DataFrame(iris.data,
columns=iris.feature_names)
data['target'] = iris.target
```

2. **Data Summary**: Let's get a quick summary of the dataset, including basic statistics like mean, median, etc.

```python
print(data.describe())  # Summary
statistics for numeric features
```

3. **Visualize Relationships**: We can visualize the relationship between the features and the target (species) using a pair plot.

```python
import seaborn as sns

# Pairplot for visualizing
relationships
sns.pairplot(data, hue='target')
plt.show()
```

4. **Visualize the Distribution of the Target**: We can also create a histogram to understand the distribution of the target variable (species).

```python
# Histogram for target variable
distribution
plt.hist(data['target'], bins=3,
color='green',
edgecolor='black')
plt.xlabel('Species')
```

```
plt.ylabel('Frequency')
plt.title('Distribution of Iris
Species')
plt.show()
```

This chapter covers how to set up a machine learning project in Python, manage data, and visualize it effectively using essential libraries like **NumPy**, **Pandas**, and **Matplotlib**. The hands-on example provides you with the basic tools to start your own data-driven machine learning project.

CHAPTER 4

Data Exploration and Preprocessing

Importance of Data Preprocessing in Machine Learning

In machine learning, **data preprocessing** is one of the most critical steps. It refers to the process of cleaning, transforming, and organizing raw data into a usable format before applying machine learning algorithms. Poor data quality can lead to incorrect model predictions, low accuracy, and overfitting, making preprocessing essential for building robust machine learning models.

Key Reasons Why Data Preprocessing is Important:

1. **Data Quality**: Raw data can contain noise, inconsistencies, or errors that need to be handled before training a model.
2. **Missing Data**: Many datasets have missing values, which can affect model performance if not addressed.
3. **Feature Scaling**: Features with different scales can affect how models learn, making it necessary to standardize or normalize them.
4. **Feature Selection**: Not all features in a dataset contribute positively to the model's prediction. Removing irrelevant features helps improve performance.
5. **Better Model Performance**: Proper preprocessing helps improve model accuracy, generalization, and convergence speed.

How to Clean and Handle Missing Data

Handling missing data is one of the first steps in data preprocessing. Incomplete data can occur for a variety of reasons, such as errors in data collection or problems in the data acquisition process.

Techniques to Handle Missing Data:

1. **Removing Missing Data**:
   - If the percentage of missing values in a feature is small, you may choose to drop rows or columns that contain missing data.

```python
# Drop rows with missing values
data.dropna(inplace=True)
```

2. **Filling Missing Data**:
   - For numerical data, you can fill missing values with the mean, median, or mode of the column.

```python
# Fill missing values with the mean of the column
data['column_name'].fillna(data['column_name'].mean(), inplace=True)
```

3. **Imputation**:
   o For more complex missing data patterns, you can use imputation techniques, such as using algorithms like KNN or regression models to predict the missing values.
4. **Forward and Backward Filling**:
   o For time-series data, you might use forward or backward filling, where missing values are filled with the previous or next available value.

```python
# Forward fill method
data.fillna(method='ffill',
inplace=True)
```

Feature Selection and Engineering: What Is It and Why It Matters?

Feature selection is the process of identifying the most relevant features (or input variables) for your machine learning model. By reducing the number of irrelevant or redundant features, you can improve the model's performance, reduce overfitting, and speed up the training process.

Why Feature Selection Matters:

• **Improves Model Accuracy**: Fewer, high-quality features reduce noise and improve the model's generalization ability.

- **Reduces Overfitting**: By removing irrelevant features, the model is less likely to memorize the noise in the data.
- **Speeds up Computation**: The fewer the features, the faster the training process.

Feature Engineering is the process of creating new features from raw data or transforming existing features to improve model performance. It involves:

1. **Creating new features**: Combining features, extracting dates, or performing mathematical operations.
2. **Transforming existing features**: For example, converting categorical variables into numeric representations (e.g., one-hot encoding).

Example: Let's say you have a dataset containing the "Date" column. You can create new features like "Day of Week" or "Month" from the "Date" column to capture temporal trends.

python

```
# Extracting new features from a date
column
data['Day_of_Week']              =
pd.to_datetime(data['Date']).dt.dayo
fweek
data['Month']                    =
pd.to_datetime(data['Date']).dt.mont
h
```

40

Normalization and Standardization of Data

In many machine learning algorithms, it's important to ensure that the features (input data) are on a similar scale. If features have different scales, the model might give more importance to features with larger values, leading to suboptimal performance.

1. **Normalization**:
    - Normalization refers to scaling the data to a fixed range, typically [0, 1].
    - It is especially important for algorithms that rely on distances, such as **K-Nearest Neighbors** (KNN) and **K-Means clustering**.
    - Formula for Min-Max Normalization: $Xnorm=X-min(X)max(X)-min(X)X\_\{n orm\} = \frac\{X \text\{min\}(X)\}\{\text\{max\}(X) \text\{min\}(X)\}Xnorm =max(X)-min(X)X-min(X)$

```python
from        sklearn.preprocessing
import MinMaxScaler

scaler = MinMaxScaler()
data[['Feature1', 'Feature2']] =
scaler.fit_transform(data[['Feat
ure1', 'Feature2']])
```

2. **Standardization**:

- o Standardization scales the data to have a mean of 0 and a standard deviation of 1.
- o This method is commonly used for algorithms like **Linear Regression**, **Logistic Regression**, and **Support Vector Machines** (SVM).
- o Formula for Standardization: $Xstd = X - \mu\sigma X\_{std} = \frac{X - \mu}{\sigma} Xstd = \sigma X - \mu$ Where $\mu\backslash mu\mu$ is the mean and $\sigma\backslash sigma\sigma$ is the standard deviation.

python

```
from        sklearn.preprocessing
import StandardScaler

scaler = StandardScaler()
data[['Feature1', 'Feature2']] =
scaler.fit_transform(data[['Feat
ure1', 'Feature2']])
```

Real-World Example: Preparing a Dataset for Model Training

Let's go through a real-world example using a dataset of house prices. We'll load the data, clean it, handle missing values, and preprocess the features.

1. **Load the Dataset**: Suppose we have a dataset with columns like "Square_Feet", "Bedrooms", "Price", and "Location".

python

```
import pandas as pd

# Load the house prices dataset
data                              =
pd.read_csv('house_prices.csv')
print(data.head())
```

2. **Handle Missing Data**: We'll drop rows with missing target values (e.g., "Price") and fill missing feature values with the mean.

python

```
# Drop rows with missing target values
(Price)
data.dropna(subset=['Price'],
inplace=True)

# Fill missing feature values with the
mean
data.fillna(data.mean(),
inplace=True)
```

3. **Feature Selection**: Let's assume we only want to use "Square_Feet" and "Bedrooms" as features to predict the "Price".

python

```
# Selecting   relevant   features   and
target
X = data[['Square_Feet', 'Bedrooms']]
y = data['Price']
```

4. **Normalization**: We'll normalize the features using Min-Max scaling to bring them into the same range.

python

```
from sklearn.preprocessing import MinMaxScaler

scaler = MinMaxScaler()
X_scaled = scaler.fit_transform(X)
```

5. **Split the Data**: Finally, we split the data into training and testing sets for model evaluation.

python

```
from sklearn.model_selection import train_test_split

X_train, X_test, y_train, y_test = train_test_split(X_scaled,          y,
test_size=0.2, random_state=42)
```

Now, the data is ready to be fed into a machine learning model!

This chapter covers essential techniques for preprocessing data, which is key to building robust machine learning models. With data cleaning, feature engineering, and scaling under your belt, you're well on your way to building powerful predictive models.

CHAPTER 5

Building Your First Machine Learning Model

Overview of the Machine Learning Workflow: From Data to Model

The machine learning workflow typically follows a structured series of steps that begin with collecting data and end with evaluating and deploying the trained model. Here's a brief overview of the common workflow:

1. **Data Collection**: The first step is gathering the dataset. This data could come from various sources, such as databases, APIs, or flat files like CSVs.
2. **Data Preprocessing**: Once the data is collected, the next step is preprocessing the data. This includes cleaning the data, handling missing values, and scaling the features.
3. **Feature Selection and Engineering**: Selecting the relevant features and potentially creating new ones through feature engineering.
4. **Splitting the Data**: The dataset is then split into training and testing sets. The training set is used to train the model, while the testing set is used to evaluate its performance.
5. **Model Selection**: Choose a machine learning algorithm suitable for your task (e.g., regression for predicting continuous values, classification for categorizing data).

6. **Model Training**: Use the training set to train the model, which involves fitting the model to the data and optimizing it through learning algorithms.

7. **Model Evaluation**: Evaluate the model's performance using the testing set. Common metrics include accuracy, precision, recall, and mean squared error (MSE), depending on the type of problem.

8. **Hyperparameter Tuning**: Adjusting hyperparameters (such as learning rate or number of trees) to improve the model's performance.

9. **Deployment**: Once the model is performing well, you can deploy it for real-world use.

Working with Supervised Learning Algorithms

Supervised learning algorithms are used when you have labeled data, meaning the target variable (the variable you want to predict) is already known. These algorithms learn from the data by mapping inputs to outputs using the labeled dataset.

Some common supervised learning algorithms include:

- **Linear Regression** (for regression tasks)
- **Logistic Regression** (for binary classification)
- **Decision Trees** (for both regression and classification)
- **Random Forests** (an ensemble method for both regression and classification)

- **Support Vector Machines (SVM)** (for classification tasks)

In this chapter, we'll focus on **Linear Regression**, which is one of the simplest and most commonly used supervised learning algorithms.

How to Split Your Data into Training and Testing Sets

Splitting the data into **training** and **testing** sets is crucial because it helps prevent overfitting. By training the model on one subset of the data (the training set) and evaluating it on another subset (the testing set), we ensure that the model can generalize well to new, unseen data.

In Python, you can use **Scikit-learn's** `train_test_split()` function to easily split the data:

```python

from sklearn.model_selection import train_test_split

# Split the data into 80% training and 20% testing
X_train, X_test, y_train, y_test = train_test_split(X, y, test_size=0.2, random_state=42)
```

- X: The feature variables.
- y: The target variable.

- `test_size`: The proportion of the data to be used for testing (usually between 0.2 and 0.3).
- `random_state`: Ensures reproducibility by controlling the random splitting.

Building Your First Regression Model with Scikit-learn

Now that you have preprocessed and split the data, you can build a regression model. We'll use **Linear Regression** to predict a continuous target variable. Linear regression tries to find the best-fitting line to model the relationship between the input features and the target variable.

Step-by-Step Code Example:

1. **Import Necessary Libraries**:

python

```
from    sklearn.linear_model    import
LinearRegression
from        sklearn.metrics        import
mean_squared_error, r2_score
import matplotlib.pyplot as plt
```

2. **Train the Linear Regression Model**:

python

```
# Initialize  the  linear  regression
model
model = LinearRegression()
```

```
# Train the model using the training
data
model.fit(X_train, y_train)
```

3. Make Predictions:

Once the model is trained, you can use it to make predictions on the testing set:

python

```
# Predict the target variable for the
testing set
y_pred = model.predict(X_test)
```

4. Evaluate the Model:

Now that you have predictions, you can evaluate the model's performance using metrics such as **Mean Squared Error (MSE)** and **R-squared**:

python

```
# Calculate the mean squared error
mse   =   mean_squared_error(y_test,
y_pred)

# Calculate R-squared value
r2 = r2_score(y_test, y_pred)

print(f"Mean Squared Error: {mse}")
print(f"R-squared: {r2}")
```

- **Mean Squared Error (MSE)**: Measures the average squared difference between the predicted and actual values. Lower values indicate better performance.
- **R-squared**: Measures the proportion of the variance in the target variable that is predictable from the features. An R-squared close to 1 means the model explains most of the variance in the data.

5. **Visualize the Results**:

Finally, you can visualize how well your model is predicting the target variable by plotting the predicted vs. actual values:

python

```
# Plotting the predicted vs actual
values
plt.scatter(y_test, y_pred)
plt.xlabel('Actual Prices')
plt.ylabel('Predicted Prices')
plt.title('Actual     vs     Predicted
Prices')
plt.show()
```

Real-World Example: Predicting Sales Based on Historical Data

Let's apply the steps we just covered to a real-world example: predicting sales based on historical data. Assume we have a dataset with features like "Ad

Spend" and "Store Visits", and the target variable is "Sales".

1. **Load the Dataset**:

python

```
import pandas as pd

# Load the sales dataset
data = pd.read_csv('sales_data.csv')
print(data.head())
```

2. **Preprocess the Data**:

Assuming the dataset has some missing values, we will clean the data:

python

```
# Fill missing values with the mean of
the respective columns
data.fillna(data.mean(),
inplace=True)
```

3. **Select Features and Target**:

Here, "Ad Spend" and "Store Visits" are the features, and "Sales" is the target variable:

python

```
X         =         data[['Ad_Spend',
'Store_Visits']]
```

```python
y = data['Sales']
```

4. **Split the Data**:

python

```python
from sklearn.model_selection import train_test_split

X_train, X_test, y_train, y_test = train_test_split(X, y, test_size=0.2, random_state=42)
```

5. **Train the Model**:

python

```python
from sklearn.linear_model import LinearRegression

model = LinearRegression()
model.fit(X_train, y_train)
```

6. **Make Predictions**:

python

```python
y_pred = model.predict(X_test)
```

7. **Evaluate the Model**:

python

```
from        sklearn.metrics        import
mean_squared_error, r2_score

mse    =    mean_squared_error(y_test,
y_pred)
r2 = r2_score(y_test, y_pred)

print(f"Mean Squared Error: {mse}")
print(f"R-squared: {r2}")
```

8. **Visualize the Results**:

```python
python

import matplotlib.pyplot as plt

plt.scatter(y_test, y_pred)
plt.xlabel('Actual Sales')
plt.ylabel('Predicted Sales')
plt.title('Actual    vs    Predicted
Sales')
plt.show()
```

This chapter introduces the basic steps involved in building a machine learning model, from splitting the data to evaluating the model's performance. By working through this example, you've learned how to apply the workflow of building a regression model using **Scikit-learn**.

CHAPTER 6

Evaluating Model Performance

Introduction to Model Evaluation Metrics: Accuracy, Precision, Recall

After building a machine learning model, the next crucial step is evaluating its performance. Evaluation metrics help us understand how well our model is making predictions and whether it's suitable for real-world use.

The evaluation metric you choose depends on the type of problem you're solving (classification, regression, etc.). Here, we'll focus on classification problems and introduce common metrics used to evaluate them:

1. **Accuracy**:
   o **Definition**: Accuracy measures the proportion of correctly predicted instances to the total number of instances.
   o **Formula**:
   Accuracy=True Positives + True Negativ esTotal Population\text{Accuracy} = \frac{\text{True Positives + True Negatives}}{\text{Total Population}}Accuracy=Total Population True Positives + True Negatives
   o **When to use**: Accuracy is a good metric when the classes in your dataset are balanced. However, it may not be reliable in imbalanced datasets.

```python
from sklearn.metrics import
accuracy_score
accuracy =
accuracy_score(y_test, y_pred)
print(f"Accuracy: {accuracy}")
```

2. **Precision**:
    - **Definition**: Precision measures the proportion of positive predictions that are actually correct. It's the ratio of true positive predictions to all positive predictions made by the model.
    - **Formula**:
      Precision=True PositivesTrue Positives + False Positives\text{Precision} = \frac{\text{True Positives}}{\text{True Positives + False Positives}}Precision=True Positives + False PositivesTrue Positives
    - **When to use**: Precision is important when the cost of false positives is high. For example, in medical diagnostics, you might want to minimize false positives (e.g., a healthy person being incorrectly diagnosed with a disease).

```python
from sklearn.metrics import
precision_score
```

```
precision                    =
precision_score(y_test, y_pred)
print(f"Precision: {precision}")
```

3. **Recall (Sensitivity)**:
   - **Definition**: Recall measures the proportion of actual positives that were correctly identified. It's the ratio of true positives to all actual positive instances in the dataset.
   - **Formula**:
     Recall=True PositivesTrue Positives + False Negatives\text{Recall} = \frac{\text{True Positives}}{\text{True Positives + False Negatives}}Recall=True Positives + False NegativesTrue Positives
   - **When to use**: Recall is crucial when the cost of false negatives is high. For example, in spam detection, you'd want to minimize false negatives (e.g., a spam email not being caught).

```
python
```

```
from sklearn.metrics import recall_score
recall = recall_score(y_test, y_pred)
print(f"Recall: {recall}")
```

Understanding the Confusion Matrix and ROC Curve

To better understand the performance of a classification model, it's helpful to look at additional metrics like the **confusion matrix** and the **ROC curve**.

1. **Confusion Matrix**:
   o The confusion matrix is a table that shows the performance of a classification model. It compares the predicted labels to the actual labels and breaks them down into four categories:
      ▪ **True Positives (TP)**: Correctly predicted positive class.
      ▪ **False Positives (FP)**: Incorrectly predicted as positive.
      ▪ **True Negatives (TN)**: Correctly predicted negative class.
      ▪ **False Negatives (FN)**: Incorrectly predicted as negative.

   The confusion matrix allows you to visualize how well your model is performing in terms of different types of errors.

```python
from sklearn.metrics import confusion_matrix
cm = confusion_matrix(y_test, y_pred)
print(cm)
```

You can also plot the confusion matrix using **Seaborn** for a more visual representation:

```python
import seaborn as sns
import matplotlib.pyplot as plt

sns.heatmap(cm, annot=True,
fmt="d", cmap="Blues",
xticklabels=["No Churn",
"Churn"], yticklabels=["No
Churn", "Churn"])
plt.xlabel("Predicted")
plt.ylabel("Actual")
plt.title("Confusion Matrix")
plt.show()
```

2. **ROC Curve (Receiver Operating Characteristic Curve)**:
    o The **ROC curve** is a graphical representation of a classification model's ability to distinguish between classes. It plots the **True Positive Rate (Recall)** against the **False Positive Rate**.
    o The area under the ROC curve (**AUC**) is used to summarize the performance of the model. An AUC score closer to 1 indicates better model performance.

```python
```

```
from     sklearn.metrics     import
roc_curve, auc

fpr,     tpr,     thresholds     =
roc_curve(y_test,
model.predict_proba(X_test)[:,1]
)
roc_auc = auc(fpr, tpr)

plt.figure()
plt.plot(fpr,                    tpr,
color="darkorange",           lw=2,
label="ROC curve (area = %0.2f)"
% roc_auc)
plt.plot([0,     1],     [0,     1],
color="navy", lw=2, linestyle="-
-")
plt.xlim([0.0, 1.0])
plt.ylim([0.0, 1.05])
plt.xlabel("False          Positive
Rate")
plt.ylabel("True Positive Rate")
plt.title("Receiver     Operating
Characteristic")
plt.legend(loc="lower right")
plt.show()
```

Techniques for Improving Model Performance

If your model is underperforming, there are several techniques you can use to improve its performance:

1. **Feature Engineering**:

- o Creating new features from existing ones or transforming features can help improve the model's performance. For example, you could create new features like "Age Group" from an age column or extract the "Day of the Week" from a date column.

2. **Hyperparameter Tuning**:
   - o Hyperparameters are parameters that you set before training the model (e.g., the number of trees in a random forest). By using techniques like **Grid Search** or **Random Search**, you can optimize these hyperparameters to improve performance.

python

```
from        sklearn.model_selection
import GridSearchCV

param_grid   =   {'n_estimators':
[10,  50,  100], 'max_depth':  [5,
10, None]}
grid_search                          =
GridSearchCV(RandomForestClassif
ier(), param_grid, cv=5)
grid_search.fit(X_train,
y_train)
print(grid_search.best_params_)
```

3. **Cross-Validation**:
   - o **Cross-validation** helps assess how the model generalizes to unseen data. It splits

the data into multiple subsets and trains the model on different combinations, which reduces the risk of overfitting.

python

```
from      sklearn.model_selection
import cross_val_score
cv_scores                =
cross_val_score(model,   X_train,
y_train, cv=5)
print(f"Cross-validation scores:
{cv_scores}")
```

4. **Ensemble Methods**:
   o Ensemble methods like **Random Forests** and **Gradient Boosting** combine multiple models to make more robust predictions, often leading to better performance.
5. **Class Imbalance Handling**:
   o In cases where the dataset has imbalanced classes (e.g., more "non-churn" than "churn"), techniques like **SMOTE (Synthetic Minority Over-sampling Technique)** or adjusting class weights can help improve model performance.

python

```
from      imblearn.over_sampling
import SMOTE
smote = SMOTE()
```

```
X_res,            y_res         =
smote.fit_resample(X_train,
y_train)
```

Real-World Example: Evaluating a Classification Model for Customer Churn Prediction

Let's consider a real-world scenario where you're building a classification model to predict whether a customer will churn (leave a service) based on their usage data.

1. **Load the Dataset**:

```python
import pandas as pd

# Load the customer churn dataset
data         =
pd.read_csv('customer_churn.csv')
print(data.head())
```

2. **Preprocess the Data**:

Handle missing values and encode categorical variables:

```python
data.fillna(data.mean(),
inplace=True)
```

```python
data['Churn'] = data['Churn'].map({'Yes': 1, 'No': 0})
```

3. Select Features and Target:

python

```python
X = data[['Age', 'Tenure', 'Monthly_Spend', 'Contract_Type']]
y = data['Churn']
```

4. Split the Data:

python

```python
from sklearn.model_selection import train_test_split

X_train, X_test, y_train, y_test = train_test_split(X, y, test_size=0.2, random_state=42)
```

5. Train a Model:

python

```python
from sklearn.ensemble import RandomForestClassifier

model = RandomForestClassifier()
model.fit(X_train, y_train)
```

6. Make Predictions:

```
python
```

```
y_pred = model.predict(X_test)
```

7. Evaluate the Model:

```
python
```

```
from        sklearn.metrics        import
accuracy_score,        precision_score,
recall_score, confusion_matrix

accuracy  =  accuracy_score(y_test,
y_pred)
precision  =  precision_score(y_test,
y_pred)
recall = recall_score(y_test, y_pred)
cm = confusion_matrix(y_test, y_pred)

print(f"Accuracy: {accuracy}")
print(f"Precision: {precision}")
print(f"Recall: {recall}")
print(f"Confusion Matrix:\n{cm}")
```

8. Plot the ROC Curve:

```
python
```

```
from        sklearn.metrics        import
roc_curve, auc

fpr,  tpr,  _  =  roc_curve(y_test,
model.predict_proba(X_test)[:,1])
roc_auc = auc(fpr, tpr)
```

```
plt.figure()
plt.plot(fpr,                    tpr,
color="darkorange", lw=2, label="ROC
curve (area = %0.2f)" % roc_auc)
plt.plot([0,      1],      [0,      1],
color="navy", lw=2, linestyle="--")
plt.xlim([0.0, 1.0])
plt.ylim([0.0, 1.05])
plt.xlabel("False Positive Rate")
plt.ylabel("True Positive Rate")
plt.title("Receiver        Operating
Characteristic")
plt.legend(loc="lower right")
plt.show()
```

In this chapter, we covered how to evaluate a classification model using key metrics like accuracy, precision, recall, confusion matrix, and ROC curve. We also explored techniques to improve model performance. By applying these metrics and techniques, you can fine-tune your model to achieve better results.

CHAPTER 7

Diving Deeper into Supervised Learning

Detailed Look at Key Algorithms: Linear Regression, Logistic Regression, and Decision Trees

Supervised learning algorithms are the backbone of many machine learning applications. These algorithms learn from labeled data, where the input features are paired with their corresponding outputs. In this chapter, we'll dive deeper into three important supervised learning algorithms: **Linear Regression**, **Logistic Regression**, and **Decision Trees**.

1. **Linear Regression**:
   o **Purpose**: Linear regression is used for regression tasks, where the goal is to predict a continuous target variable.
   o **How it works**: Linear regression models the relationship between input features and a continuous target variable by fitting a linear equation to the data.
   o **Formula**: $y=\beta 0+\beta 1x1+\beta 2x2+...+\beta nxny = \beta\_0 + \beta\_1x\_1 + \beta\_2x\_2 + ... + \beta\_nx\_ny=\beta 0+\beta 1x1+\beta 2x2+...+\beta nxn$
      Where:
      ▪ yyy is the predicted output (dependent variable),
      ▪ $x1,x2,...,xnx\_1, x\_2, ..., x\_nx1,x2,...,xn$ are the input features (independent variables),

- $\beta 0 \backslash beta\_0 \beta 0$ is the intercept, and $\beta 1, \beta 2, ..., \beta n \backslash beta\_1, \backslash beta\_2, ..., \backslash beta\_n \beta 1, \beta 2, ..., \beta n$ are the coefficients.
  - **Applications**: Predicting house prices, stock prices, or any other continuous numeric value.

python

```
from sklearn.linear_model import
LinearRegression
model = LinearRegression()
model.fit(X_train, y_train)
y_pred = model.predict(X_test)
```

2. **Logistic Regression**:
   - **Purpose**: Logistic regression is used for classification tasks, particularly when the target variable is binary (e.g., 0 or 1, True or False).
   - **How it works**: Unlike linear regression, logistic regression uses the **logistic function** (also known as the sigmoid function) to map any real-valued number into a probability between 0 and 1, which can then be mapped to a class label.
   - **Formula**:
     $p(y=1|x) = \frac{1}{1+e^{-(\beta 0+\beta 1 x 1+\beta 2 x 2+...+\beta n x n)}}$ $p(y=1|x) = \frac{1}{1 + e^{-(\beta\_0 + \beta\_1 x\_1 + \beta\_2 x\_2 + ... + \beta\_n x\_n)}} p(y=1|x) = \frac{1}{1+e^{-(\beta 0+\beta 1 x 1 +\beta 2 x 2+...+\beta n x n)}}$ Where:

- $p(y=1|x)p(y=1|x)p(y=1|x)$ is the probability that the target yyy equals 1 given the input features xxx.
  - **Applications**: Spam email classification, customer churn prediction, medical diagnosis (e.g., predicting the likelihood of a disease).

```python
from sklearn.linear_model import
LogisticRegression
model = LogisticRegression()
model.fit(X_train, y_train)
y_pred = model.predict(X_test)
```

3. **Decision Trees**:
   - **Purpose**: Decision trees are versatile algorithms that can be used for both classification and regression tasks.
   - **How it works**: Decision trees split the data into subsets based on the most significant feature at each node. These splits continue recursively to create a tree-like structure, with each leaf node representing a predicted class or value.
   - **Applications**: Customer segmentation, loan default prediction, image classification, etc.
   - **Advantages**: Easy to interpret and visualize, no need for feature scaling.

- o **Disadvantages**: Prone to overfitting, especially with deep trees.

python

```
from       sklearn.tree       import
DecisionTreeClassifier
model = DecisionTreeClassifier()
model.fit(X_train, y_train)
y_pred = model.predict(X_test)
```

Practical Example: Building a Spam Classifier Using Logistic Regression

Let's build a spam classifier using **Logistic Regression** to predict whether an email is spam or not based on features like word frequency, message length, and other text-based features. We'll use the **SMS Spam Collection Dataset**, which contains SMS messages labeled as either "spam" or "ham" (non-spam).

1. **Load and Preprocess the Dataset**:

python

```
import pandas as pd

# Load the SMS Spam Collection dataset
data     =     pd.read_csv('spam.csv',
encoding='latin-1')
print(data.head())
```

2. **Preprocess the Text Data**:

- Text data needs to be cleaned and transformed into a numerical format for machine learning algorithms. We'll start by removing unnecessary columns and transforming the text into a vector of numbers using **CountVectorizer** or **TF-IDF** (Term Frequency-Inverse Document Frequency).

python

```python
from sklearn.feature_extraction.text
import CountVectorizer

# Drop unnecessary columns
data = data[['v1', 'v2']]
data.columns = ['label', 'message']

# Convert labels to binary values
(spam = 1, ham = 0)
data['label']                       =
data['label'].map({'spam': 1, 'ham':
0})

# Convert text messages into a bag-
of-words model using CountVectorizer
vectorizer                          =
CountVectorizer(stop_words='english'
)
X                                   =
vectorizer.fit_transform(data['messa
ge'])
```

```
# Labels
y = data['label']
```

3. Split the Data:

We'll now split the data into training and testing sets.

```
python

from sklearn.model_selection import
train_test_split

X_train, X_test, y_train, y_test =
train_test_split(X, y, test_size=0.2,
random_state=42)
```

4. Train the Logistic Regression Model:

Now, we can train the logistic regression model using the training data.

```
python

from sklearn.linear_model import
LogisticRegression

model = LogisticRegression()
model.fit(X_train, y_train)
```

5. Make Predictions:

Let's predict whether the emails in the test set are spam or ham.

```python
```

```python
y_pred = model.predict(X_test)
```

6. Evaluate the Model:

Now, we'll evaluate the model's performance using accuracy, precision, recall, and the confusion matrix.

```python
```

```python
from sklearn.metrics import accuracy_score, precision_score, recall_score, confusion_matrix

accuracy = accuracy_score(y_test, y_pred)
precision = precision_score(y_test, y_pred)
recall = recall_score(y_test, y_pred)
cm = confusion_matrix(y_test, y_pred)

print(f"Accuracy: {accuracy}")
print(f"Precision: {precision}")
print(f"Recall: {recall}")
print(f"Confusion Matrix:\n{cm}")
```

7. Visualize the Confusion Matrix:

Visualizing the confusion matrix helps us understand the classification performance more clearly.

```python
```

```
import seaborn as sns
import matplotlib.pyplot as plt

sns.heatmap(cm, annot=True, fmt="d",
cmap="Blues", xticklabels=["Ham",
"Spam"], yticklabels=["Ham", "Spam"])
plt.xlabel("Predicted")
plt.ylabel("Actual")
plt.title("Confusion Matrix")
plt.show()
```

Exploring Different Types of Supervised Learning Tasks: Regression vs. Classification

Supervised learning tasks can generally be broken down into two broad categories:

1. **Regression**:
   - **Purpose**: The goal in regression is to predict a continuous target variable based on the input features.
   - **Example**: Predicting house prices, stock prices, or any other continuous value.
   - **Algorithms Used**: Linear Regression, Polynomial Regression, Decision Trees (for regression), Random Forests, and Support Vector Machines (SVM) for regression.
   - **Evaluation Metrics**: Mean Squared Error (MSE), Mean Absolute Error (MAE), R-squared.
2. **Classification**:

- o **Purpose**: The goal in classification is to predict discrete labels or categories. For example, classifying an email as either spam or ham.
- o **Example**: Identifying whether an image is of a cat or dog, diagnosing diseases as positive or negative, or classifying customer churn.
- o **Algorithms Used**: Logistic Regression, Decision Trees, Random Forests, K-Nearest Neighbors (KNN), Support Vector Machines (SVM).
- o **Evaluation Metrics**: Accuracy, Precision, Recall, F1-score, Confusion Matrix, ROC Curve.

This chapter has provided a detailed look into key supervised learning algorithms, including **Linear Regression**, **Logistic Regression**, and **Decision Trees**. We also worked through a practical example of building a spam classifier using logistic regression, and explored the key differences between regression and classification tasks in machine learning.

CHAPTER 8

Exploring Unsupervised Learning

What is Unsupervised Learning?

Unsupervised learning is a type of machine learning where the algorithm is provided with data that has no labeled responses. The goal of unsupervised learning is to uncover hidden patterns or structures in the data without the guidance of a target variable. Unlike supervised learning, where each input comes with a corresponding label, unsupervised learning tries to find inherent relationships or groupings in the data on its own.

Key areas where unsupervised learning is used:

- **Clustering**: Grouping similar data points together.
- **Dimensionality Reduction**: Reducing the number of features while preserving important patterns in the data.

Common unsupervised learning algorithms include:

- **Clustering algorithms** (e.g., K-Means, DBSCAN)
- **Dimensionality Reduction algorithms** (e.g., PCA, t-SNE)

Introduction to Clustering and Dimensionality Reduction

1. **Clustering**:
   - Clustering is the process of grouping data points such that data points within a group (cluster) are more similar to each other than to those in other groups. The idea is to segment the dataset into distinct groups that have similar characteristics.
   - **Applications**: Market segmentation, customer profiling, image segmentation, anomaly detection.
   - **Popular Clustering Algorithms**:
     - **K-Means**: Divides the data into K clusters by minimizing the variance within clusters.
     - **Hierarchical Clustering**: Builds a tree-like structure of clusters.
     - **DBSCAN (Density-Based Spatial Clustering of Applications with Noise)**: Identifies clusters based on density, which is useful for clusters of arbitrary shapes.
2. **Dimensionality Reduction**:
   - Dimensionality reduction involves reducing the number of features (or dimensions) in a dataset while preserving as much of the variability as possible. This is useful when dealing with high-dimensional data, which can be difficult to visualize and process.

- o **Applications**: Feature selection, data visualization, noise reduction.
- o **Popular Dimensionality Reduction Algorithms**:
  - **Principal Component Analysis (PCA)**: A technique that transforms data into a new coordinate system to maximize the variance along the principal axes.
  - **t-SNE**: A technique for visualizing high-dimensional data by reducing it to two or three dimensions.

Hands-on with K-Means Clustering for Customer Segmentation

Let's apply **K-Means clustering** to segment customers based on their purchasing behavior. The K-Means algorithm will help us group customers into clusters based on similarities in their features.

Step-by-Step Code Example:

1. **Load the Dataset**:

For this example, let's assume we have a dataset containing features like Annual Income, Spending Score, and Age for a set of customers.

```python
import pandas as pd
```

```
# Load a dataset of customer data
(e.g., annual income and spending
score)
data                          =
pd.read_csv('customer_data.csv')
print(data.head())
```

2. **Preprocess the Data**:

Before applying clustering, we need to select the relevant features and possibly scale them to ensure they're on the same scale. K-Means is sensitive to the scale of the data, so it's important to standardize the features.

```python

from sklearn.preprocessing import
StandardScaler

# Select relevant features (e.g.,
Annual Income and Spending Score)
X        =        data[['Annual_Income',
'Spending_Score']]

# Standardize the features
scaler = StandardScaler()
X_scaled = scaler.fit_transform(X)
```

3. **Apply K-Means Clustering**:

Let's apply K-Means clustering with 3 clusters. The number of clusters (K) is a hyperparameter that can be selected based on the problem, domain knowledge, or by using techniques like the **elbow method**.

```python

from sklearn.cluster import KMeans

# Apply K-Means clustering with 3 clusters
kmeans     =     KMeans(n_clusters=3, random_state=42)
kmeans.fit(X_scaled)

# Get the cluster labels for each customer
data['Cluster'] = kmeans.labels_
```

4. **Visualize the Clusters**:

Now that we've assigned each customer to a cluster, we can visualize the clusters.

```python

import matplotlib.pyplot as plt

# Scatter plot to visualize the clusters
plt.scatter(data['Annual_Income'],
data['Spending_Score'],
c=data['Cluster'], cmap='viridis')
plt.xlabel('Annual Income')
plt.ylabel('Spending Score')
```

```
plt.title('Customer Segmentation (K-
Means Clustering)')
plt.show()
```

In this plot, each customer is color-coded according to the cluster they belong to. You should see distinct groups of customers, which could correspond to different customer segments, such as high-income, high-spending customers, or low-income, low-spending customers.

Understanding Principal Component Analysis (PCA) for Feature Reduction

PCA is a technique for **dimensionality reduction** that helps in reducing the number of features in your dataset while retaining the most important information (variance). This is useful when you have high-dimensional data and want to reduce it for better visualization or faster model training.

1. **How PCA Works**:
    - PCA projects the data into a new set of dimensions (principal components) ordered by the amount of variance they capture from the original data. The first principal component captures the most variance, the second one captures the second-most, and so on.
    - The number of principal components can be chosen based on how much variance you want to preserve.
2. **Step-by-Step Code Example**:

Let's apply **PCA** to reduce the dimensionality of the dataset. For this example, we'll assume the data contains multiple features, and we'll reduce it to two principal components for visualization.

```python
from sklearn.decomposition import PCA

# Apply PCA to reduce the data to 2
components
pca = PCA(n_components=2)
X_pca = pca.fit_transform(X_scaled)

# Create a new DataFrame with the
principal components
data_pca      =      pd.DataFrame(X_pca,
columns=['PC1', 'PC2'])

# Visualize the data in the reduced 2D
space
plt.scatter(data_pca['PC1'],
data_pca['PC2'])
plt.xlabel('Principal Component 1')
plt.ylabel('Principal Component 2')
plt.title('PCA of Customer Data')
plt.show()
```

3. **Explained Variance**:

You can check how much variance each principal component explains to understand how well the data is represented by the reduced dimensions.

```python
print(f"Explained            Variance:
{pca.explained_variance_ratio_}")
```

This tells you the proportion of the dataset's variance that each principal component captures. For example, if the first component explains 80% of the variance and the second component explains 15%, together they capture 95% of the variance, meaning you can represent the data quite well with just two components.

Summary

In this chapter, we covered the fundamentals of **Unsupervised Learning** and its two major components: **Clustering** and **Dimensionality Reduction**. We implemented **K-Means clustering** to segment customers based on their income and spending scores, and we used **Principal Component Analysis (PCA)** to reduce the dimensionality of a dataset while retaining important features.

CHAPTER SUMMARY:

- **Clustering** is used to group similar data points together. **K-Means** is one of the most popular algorithms for clustering.
- **PCA** helps reduce the number of features in a dataset while retaining as much variance as

possible, making it easier to visualize and process high-dimensional data.

- **Unsupervised learning** techniques like clustering and dimensionality reduction are powerful tools for discovering patterns and simplifying complex datasets.

CHAPTER 9

Introduction to Neural Networks

What Are Neural Networks and Why They Matter?

Neural Networks are a subset of machine learning algorithms inspired by the structure and functioning of the human brain. They are designed to recognize patterns and can learn from data in a way that mimics human decision-making processes. Neural networks are particularly powerful in tasks such as image recognition, speech processing, and natural language understanding.

In simple terms, a neural network is a series of algorithms that try to recognize underlying relationships in a set of data through a process that mimics the way the human brain operates. By adjusting weights through a process called **training**, neural networks are able to improve their predictions or classifications.

Neural networks are essential in:

- **Deep Learning**: When neural networks have many layers (deep neural networks), they can model complex, non-linear relationships in data.
- **Complex Data**: Neural networks are extremely powerful when dealing with high-dimensional data, such as images, audio, and text.
- **Real-world Applications**: They power technologies like self-driving cars, facial

recognition, speech assistants, and language translation.

Basic Components of a Neural Network: Neurons, Layers, Activation Functions

A neural network is composed of three key components: **neurons**, **layers**, and **activation functions**.

1. **Neurons**:
   o A **neuron** is the basic unit of a neural network. It receives input, processes it, and produces an output. Neurons are arranged in layers, and each neuron in one layer connects to neurons in the next layer through **weights**.
   o Each neuron performs a simple mathematical operation on the inputs and passes the result through an activation function.
2. **Layers**:
   o A neural network consists of three types of layers:
      1. **Input Layer**: This layer receives the input data. Each neuron represents one feature.
      2. **Hidden Layers**: These layers process the data by performing weighted summation and passing it through an activation function.
      3. **Output Layer**: The final layer produces the result. In classification, this could represent

the probabilities for different classes.

o The depth of the network (i.e., the number of hidden layers) is what makes a neural network "deep," and this is what enables the network to learn highly complex patterns.

3. **Activation Functions**:

o **Activation functions** determine whether a neuron should be activated or not, i.e., whether the information that the neuron is processing is relevant enough to be passed to the next layer.

o Common activation functions:

- **Sigmoid**: Maps the input to a range between 0 and 1. Often used in binary classification tasks.

- **ReLU (Rectified Linear Unit)**: Returns 0 for negative inputs and the input itself for positive inputs. It's widely used in hidden layers because of its ability to help with faster training and better performance.

- **Softmax**: Converts the output into a probability distribution, typically used in multi-class classification problems.

Sigmoid Example:

$f(x) = \frac{1}{1 + e^{-x}}$

ReLU Example:

$f(x)=\max(0,x)f(x) = \max(0, x)f(x)=\max(0,x)$

Building a Simple Neural Network from Scratch in Python

Let's walk through building a simple **feedforward neural network** using **Python**. This network will have one input layer, one hidden layer, and one output layer. We'll implement it from scratch to understand the key concepts of neural networks.

1. **Import Necessary Libraries**:

python

```
import numpy as np
```

2. **Create the Neural Network Class**:

We'll define a simple neural network with one hidden layer. The network will use **Sigmoid** activation for simplicity.

python

```
class SimpleNeuralNetwork:
    def __init__(self, input_size,
hidden_size, output_size):
        # Initialize weights with
random values
        self.input_size = input_size
```

```
        self.hidden_size        =
hidden_size
        self.output_size        =
output_size

        # Weight matrices
        self.W1                 =
np.random.randn(self.input_size,
self.hidden_size)  # Weights for input
to hidden
        self.W2                 =
np.random.randn(self.hidden_size,
self.output_size)    #  Weights  for
hidden to output

        # Biases
        self.b1    =    np.zeros((1,
self.hidden_size))
        self.b2    =    np.zeros((1,
self.output_size))

    def sigmoid(self, x):
        return 1 / (1 + np.exp(-x))

    def sigmoid_derivative(self, x):
        return x * (1 - x)

    def forward(self, X):
        #  Forward  pass:  input  to
hidden layer
        self.hidden_input = np.dot(X,
self.W1) + self.b1
```

```python
        self.hidden_output        =
self.sigmoid(self.hidden_input)

        # Forward pass: hidden to
output layer
        self.final_input          =
np.dot(self.hidden_output, self.W2) +
self.b2
        self.final_output         =
self.sigmoid(self.final_input)

        return self.final_output

    def backward(self, X, y,
learning_rate=0.01):
        # Backpropagation
        output_error    =    y    -
self.final_output
        output_delta = output_error *
self.sigmoid_derivative(self.final_o
utput)

        hidden_error              =
output_delta.dot(self.W2.T)
        hidden_delta = hidden_error *
self.sigmoid_derivative(self.hidden_
output)

        # Update weights and biases
using the gradient descent algorithm
        self.W1                  +=
X.T.dot(hidden_delta) * learning_rate
```

```python
        self.W2                    +=
self.hidden_output.T.dot(output_delt
a) * learning_rate
        self.b1                    +=
np.sum(hidden_delta,     axis=0)    *
learning_rate
        self.b2                    +=
np.sum(output_delta,     axis=0)    *
learning_rate

    def     train(self,     X,     y,
epochs=10000, learning_rate=0.01):
        for epoch in range(epochs):
            self.forward(X)
            self.backward(X,        y,
learning_rate)
            if epoch % 1000 == 0:
                loss            =
np.mean(np.square(y              -
self.final_output))   # Mean Squared
Error
                print(f"Epoch
{epoch}: Loss = {loss}")
```

3. **Train the Neural Network**:

Let's use a simple dataset for a binary classification problem (e.g., predicting whether a student passed or failed based on their study hours).

```python
python
```

```python
# Sample data: [Hours studied, Hours
slept], Target: 0 = Fail, 1 = Pass
```

```
X = np.array([[5, 2], [8, 3], [7, 4],
[6, 5], [4, 6]])
y = np.array([[1], [1], [1], [0],
[0]])

# Initialize and train the neural
network
nn                                =
SimpleNeuralNetwork(input_size=2,
hidden_size=3, output_size=1)
nn.train(X, y)
```

This simple neural network will learn to predict whether a student passes or fails based on their study hours and sleep hours.

Real-World Example: Simple Image Classification with Neural Networks

Let's now look at a more practical example—building a **simple image classifier** using a neural network. For simplicity, we'll use a dataset like the **MNIST dataset**, which contains handwritten digits (0-9). The goal is to classify images of digits into the correct category.

1. **Load the Dataset**: We'll use **Keras**, a high-level neural network library, to load and preprocess the dataset.

```python
python
```

```python
from tensorflow.keras.datasets import
mnist
from  tensorflow.keras.utils  import
to_categorical

# Load MNIST dataset
(X_train,  y_train),  (X_test,  y_test)
= mnist.load_data()

# Flatten the images from 28x28 to 784
(28 * 28) pixels
X_train                          =
X_train.reshape(X_train.shape[0],
784)
X_test                           =
X_test.reshape(X_test.shape[0],  784)

# Normalize  the  pixel  values  to  be
between 0 and 1
X_train = X_train / 255.0
X_test = X_test / 255.0

# One-hot encode the labels
y_train = to_categorical(y_train, 10)
y_test = to_categorical(y_test, 10)
```

2. Build the Neural Network Model:

```python
python

from  tensorflow.keras.models  import
Sequential
from  tensorflow.keras.layers  import
Dense
```

```python
# Build the neural network model
model = Sequential()
model.add(Dense(128,    input_dim=784,
activation='relu'))    # Hidden layer
with 128 neurons
model.add(Dense(10,
activation='softmax'))        # Output
layer with 10 neurons (one for each
class)

# Compile the model
model.compile(optimizer='adam',
loss='categorical_crossentropy',
metrics=['accuracy'])
```

3. **Train the Model**:

```python
python
```

```python
# Train the model on the training data
model.fit(X_train, y_train, epochs=5,
batch_size=32, verbose=2)
```

4. **Evaluate the Model**:

```python
python
```

```python
# Evaluate the model on the test data
loss,            accuracy            =
model.evaluate(X_test, y_test)
print(f"Test Loss: {loss}")
print(f"Test Accuracy: {accuracy}")
```

Summary

In this chapter, we introduced **Neural Networks**, explaining their structure and importance in machine learning. We built a simple neural network from scratch to predict binary outcomes and explored how **activation functions**, **layers**, and **neurons** work together. We also implemented a **real-world example** using the **MNIST dataset** for image classification.

CHAPTER SUMMARY:

- Neural networks are powerful tools for tasks such as image recognition and speech processing.
- Understanding the components of a neural network, including neurons, layers, and activation functions, is essential to building and tuning models.
- Neural networks can be built from scratch for simpler tasks, but more complex tasks, like image classification, benefit from deep learning frameworks like **Keras** or **TensorFlow**.

CHAPTER 10

Deep Learning and Deep Neural Networks

Overview of Deep Learning vs. Machine Learning

Deep learning and machine learning are closely related, but they differ significantly in terms of the complexity of the models and the types of problems they can solve.

1. **Machine Learning (ML)**:
   - In traditional machine learning, algorithms learn from data through explicit programming and feature engineering. The focus is on identifying patterns in the data and building a model using those patterns.
   - Common machine learning algorithms include **linear regression, logistic regression, decision trees, support vector machines**, and **K-nearest neighbors**.
   - Machine learning models typically require manual feature extraction, where domain knowledge is used to identify the most relevant features to train the model.
   - **Use cases**: Predicting house prices, classifying emails as spam or not, and predicting customer churn.
2. **Deep Learning (DL)**:
   - Deep learning is a subset of machine learning, where neural networks with many layers (hence "deep" learning) are

used to automatically learn from large amounts of data. Deep learning models are capable of learning complex representations from raw data.

- Unlike traditional machine learning, deep learning does not require explicit feature engineering. The model automatically learns relevant features through its layers.
- **Deep Neural Networks (DNNs)** are used for deep learning, where each layer consists of many neurons that transform data before passing it to the next layer.
- **Use cases**: Image recognition, speech recognition, natural language processing (NLP), and autonomous driving.

Key Differences:

- **Data requirements**: Deep learning requires large amounts of data for training, while traditional machine learning can work with smaller datasets.
- **Model complexity**: Deep learning models are more complex and have more parameters to tune, whereas machine learning models are relatively simpler.
- **Feature engineering**: Deep learning automates the process of feature extraction, while traditional machine learning relies on manually crafted features.

The Architecture of Deep Neural Networks

Deep neural networks (DNNs) consist of multiple layers of neurons, which enable them to learn complex patterns from data. Each layer in a deep network transforms the data in such a way that higher layers learn more abstract representations.

Key Components of a Deep Neural Network:

1. **Input Layer**: This is the first layer where the raw data enters the network. Each neuron in this layer corresponds to one feature in the input data.
2. **Hidden Layers**: These are intermediate layers between the input and output. Each neuron in the hidden layers performs calculations on the input data and passes it to the next layer. DNNs have many hidden layers, allowing them to learn complex patterns.
3. **Output Layer**: This layer produces the final output. In a classification problem, it will output the probability of each class (using an activation function like **Softmax**).
4. **Activation Functions**: These functions introduce non-linearity in the network, allowing it to learn more complex patterns. Common activation functions are **ReLU** (Rectified Linear Unit), **Sigmoid**, and **Tanh**.
5. **Weights and Biases**: Each connection between neurons has an associated weight that represents the strength of the connection. Biases are added to adjust the output of the neurons. Both weights

and biases are learned during the training process.

6. **Loss Function**: This function measures how well the network's predictions match the actual labels. During training, the model adjusts its weights to minimize the loss function.

7. **Backpropagation**: This is the process of adjusting weights using the **gradient descent** optimization algorithm. It propagates the error back through the network to update the weights and reduce the error.

Introduction to TensorFlow and Keras for Deep Learning

TensorFlow is an open-source deep learning framework developed by Google. It provides comprehensive tools for building, training, and deploying deep learning models. **Keras** is a high-level API built on top of TensorFlow, designed to make it easier to build and experiment with deep learning models.

TensorFlow provides:

- **TensorFlow Core**: A flexible framework for building models from scratch.
- **Keras API**: A user-friendly, high-level API for building deep learning models quickly.

Why Use TensorFlow and Keras?:

- TensorFlow is widely used for building scalable deep learning models and deploying them on various platforms (e.g., web, mobile, cloud).
- Keras makes it simple to prototype deep learning models with less code, which is particularly helpful for beginners and researchers.

Let's walk through an example of how to build a deep neural network using **TensorFlow** and **Keras**.

Hands-on: Building a Deep Neural Network for Handwritten Digit Recognition (MNIST Dataset)

In this example, we'll use the **MNIST dataset**, which contains images of handwritten digits (0-9), and we'll build a neural network to classify these digits.

1. **Import Necessary Libraries**:

python

```python
import tensorflow as tf
from tensorflow.keras.models import Sequential
from tensorflow.keras.layers import Dense, Flatten
from tensorflow.keras.datasets import mnist
from tensorflow.keras.utils import to_categorical
```

2. **Load and Preprocess the MNIST Dataset**:

The MNIST dataset comes prepackaged with Keras. We'll load the data, normalize the pixel values, and convert the labels to one-hot encoding.

python

```
# Load the MNIST dataset
(X_train, y_train), (X_test, y_test)
= mnist.load_data()

# Normalize pixel values to be between
0 and 1
X_train = X_train / 255.0
X_test = X_test / 255.0

# Flatten the images from 28x28 to 784
(28 * 28) pixels
X_train                              =
X_train.reshape(X_train.shape[0],
784)
X_test                               =
X_test.reshape(X_test.shape[0], 784)

# One-hot encode the labels
y_train = to_categorical(y_train, 10)
y_test = to_categorical(y_test, 10)
```

3. **Build the Neural Network Model**:

We'll use a simple **feedforward neural network** with one hidden layer.

python

```python
# Build the model
model = Sequential()

# Input layer: Flatten the 28x28 image
into a 784-dimensional vector
model.add(Flatten(input_shape=(784,)
))

# Hidden layer: 128 neurons with ReLU
activation
model.add(Dense(128,
activation='relu'))

# Output layer: 10 neurons for the 10
classes (digits 0-9) with softmax
activation
model.add(Dense(10,
activation='softmax'))

# Compile the model: Using Adam
optimizer and categorical
crossentropy loss
model.compile(optimizer='adam',
loss='categorical_crossentropy',
metrics=['accuracy'])
```

4. **Train the Model**:

We'll train the model on the MNIST training set for 5 epochs.

```python
python
```

```python
# Train the model
```

```
model.fit(X_train, y_train, epochs=5,
batch_size=32)
```

5. **Evaluate the Model**:

After training, we can evaluate the model on the test data to see how well it performs.

python

```
# Evaluate the model on the test set
loss,           accuracy           =
model.evaluate(X_test, y_test)
print(f"Test Loss: {loss}")
print(f"Test Accuracy: {accuracy}")
```

6. **Make Predictions**:

Once the model is trained, we can use it to predict handwritten digits.

python

```
# Make predictions on the test set
predictions = model.predict(X_test)

# Display the predicted label for the
first test image
import numpy as np
print(f"Predicted           Label:
{np.argmax(predictions[0])}")
```

Summary

In this chapter, we introduced **Deep Learning** and **Deep Neural Networks**, discussing how they differ from traditional machine learning. We covered the architecture of deep neural networks, including **input**, **hidden**, and **output layers**, and the role of **activation functions** in learning complex patterns.

We also introduced **TensorFlow** and **Keras**, two powerful libraries for building deep learning models, and walked through a hands-on example of building a deep neural network for **handwritten digit recognition** using the **MNIST dataset**.

CHAPTER SUMMARY:

- Deep learning allows neural networks with many layers to learn complex patterns from data.
- **TensorFlow** and **Keras** provide powerful tools for building and deploying deep learning models.
- Building a neural network with **Keras** is fast and efficient, making it an excellent choice for deep learning practitioners.

CHAPTER 11

Convolutional Neural Networks (CNNs) for Computer Vision

What is a Convolutional Neural Network (CNN)?

A **Convolutional Neural Network (CNN)** is a specialized type of deep neural network designed for processing structured grid-like data, such as images. CNNs are widely used in **computer vision** tasks like image classification, object detection, facial recognition, and more due to their ability to capture spatial hierarchies and patterns in data.

CNNs differ from regular neural networks in that they apply **convolutional layers** to input data, allowing them to automatically detect patterns such as edges, shapes, textures, and objects from raw pixel values.

Key Features of CNNs:

- **Local Receptive Fields**: Instead of connecting every neuron to every other neuron (as in fully connected layers), CNNs use **local receptive fields** to process small portions of the input (e.g., small patches of an image). This reduces the number of parameters and computational complexity.
- **Weight Sharing**: Filters (or kernels) are applied across the entire image, meaning the same weights are shared across different parts of the

input, further reducing the number of parameters.

- **Pooling**: Pooling layers help reduce the spatial dimensions of the data, allowing the network to focus on high-level features and improving computational efficiency.

Understanding Convolution, Pooling, and Fully Connected Layers

1. **Convolution**:
   o In the convolutional layer, a small filter (or kernel) slides over the input image and performs an element-wise multiplication followed by a summation. This process extracts local features like edges, textures, and patterns.
   o **Convolution Operation**:
     - Suppose you have an image and a 3x3 filter. The filter slides across the image, performing the following:
       1. Multiply the filter values with the corresponding pixel values of the image.
       2. Sum the products and place the result in the output feature map.
   o **Stride**: The step size at which the filter moves across the image.
   o **Padding**: Adding extra pixels around the image to ensure that the filter can fully

cover the image, preserving spatial dimensions.

2. **Pooling**:
   - Pooling layers reduce the spatial dimensions of the input, making the model more computationally efficient and helping to reduce overfitting.
   - **Max Pooling**: This is the most common type of pooling, where the maximum value from a patch of the image is selected.
   - **Average Pooling**: This is an alternative where the average value from a patch of the image is selected.
   - **Example**: A 2x2 max pooling operation selects the maximum value from each 2x2 region of the image.

3. **Fully Connected Layers**:
   - After the convolution and pooling layers, CNNs usually have one or more fully connected layers, which connect every neuron in one layer to every neuron in the next layer.
   - These layers help classify the learned features into different categories.
   - **Flattening**: The output of the convolutional and pooling layers is flattened into a 1D vector before feeding it into the fully connected layers.

Building a CNN Model for Image Classification with Keras

Let's walk through the steps of building a simple **Convolutional Neural Network** using **Keras** to classify images. For simplicity, we'll use the **CIFAR-10 dataset**, which contains 60,000 32x32 color images in 10 classes.

1. **Import Necessary Libraries**:

python

```python
import tensorflow as tf
from tensorflow.keras.models import Sequential
from tensorflow.keras.layers import Conv2D, MaxPooling2D, Flatten, Dense
from tensorflow.keras.datasets import cifar10
from tensorflow.keras.utils import to_categorical
```

2. **Load and Preprocess the CIFAR-10 Dataset**:

The CIFAR-10 dataset contains images of 10 different classes, such as airplanes, cats, dogs, etc. We'll load the data, normalize it, and one-hot encode the labels.

python

```python
# Load the CIFAR-10 dataset
```

```
(X_train, y_train), (X_test, y_test)
= cifar10.load_data()
```

```
# Normalize the pixel values to be
between 0 and 1
X_train = X_train / 255.0
X_test = X_test / 255.0
```

```
# One-hot encode the labels
y_train = to_categorical(y_train, 10)
y_test = to_categorical(y_test, 10)
```

3. **Build the CNN Model**:

Now, let's define a simple CNN model with two convolutional layers followed by max-pooling, then flattening, and two fully connected layers for classification.

```
python
```

```
model = Sequential()
```

```
# Convolutional layer with 32 filters
of size 3x3, followed by ReLU
activation
model.add(Conv2D(32, (3, 3),
activation='relu', input_shape=(32,
32, 3)))
```

```
# Max pooling layer
model.add(MaxPooling2D(pool_size=(2,
2)))
```

```python
# Another convolutional layer with 64
filters and ReLU activation
model.add(Conv2D(64,        (3,        3),
activation='relu'))

# Another max pooling layer
model.add(MaxPooling2D(pool_size=(2,
2)))

# Flatten   the   output   from   the
convolutional layers
model.add(Flatten())

# Fully   connected   layer   with   128
neurons and ReLU activation
model.add(Dense(128,
activation='relu'))

# Output layer with 10 neurons (one
for each class) and softmax activation
model.add(Dense(10,
activation='softmax'))
```

4. **Compile the Model**:

Now we'll compile the model, specifying the optimizer, loss function, and evaluation metrics.

```python
python
```

```python
# Compile the model
model.compile(optimizer='adam',
loss='categorical_crossentropy',
metrics=['accuracy'])
```

5. **Train the Model**:

We'll now train the model using the training data for 10 epochs.

python

```
# Train the model
model.fit(X_train,          y_train,
epochs=10,           batch_size=64,
validation_data=(X_test, y_test))
```

6. **Evaluate the Model**:

After training, we can evaluate the model's performance on the test data.

python

```
# Evaluate the model on the test set
loss,         accuracy         =
model.evaluate(X_test, y_test)
print(f"Test Loss: {loss}")
print(f"Test Accuracy: {accuracy}")
```

Real-World Example: Object Detection in Images

While image classification assigns labels to entire images, **object detection** involves locating and classifying multiple objects within an image. A common approach for object detection is the **YOLO (You Only Look Once)** algorithm, which divides an image into a grid and predicts bounding boxes and class probabilities for each grid cell.

Here's a high-level overview of how to perform object detection using CNNs:

1. **Input**: The input is an image containing one or more objects.
2. **CNN Layers**: The image is passed through a series of convolutional layers to extract features at different scales.
3. **Bounding Box Prediction**: The model predicts bounding boxes for each object in the image. Each bounding box has 4 coordinates (x, y, width, height).
4. **Class Prediction**: For each bounding box, the model predicts the class of the object contained within the box.
5. **Non-Maximum Suppression (NMS)**: This technique is used to eliminate duplicate bounding boxes for the same object by keeping the box with the highest confidence score.

Important Considerations:

- **Anchor Boxes**: Predefined bounding boxes that help the model detect objects of different shapes and sizes.
- **IoU (Intersection over Union)**: A metric used to evaluate how well predicted bounding boxes overlap with ground truth boxes.

In practice, object detection is more complex and requires using pre-trained models and techniques like **Faster R-CNN, YOLO**, or **SSD (Single Shot Multibox Detector)** for accurate results.

112

Summary

In this chapter, we covered **Convolutional Neural Networks (CNNs)**, which are specialized neural networks for processing image data. We explained the key components of CNNs, including **convolution**, **pooling**, and **fully connected layers**, and built a simple CNN for image classification using the **CIFAR-10 dataset**.

CHAPTER SUMMARY:

- CNNs are essential for computer vision tasks because they automatically detect spatial hierarchies and patterns in images.
- Convolutional layers help detect local features, pooling layers reduce dimensionality, and fully connected layers classify the learned features.
- Using frameworks like **Keras** and **TensorFlow**, building and training CNNs for image classification is straightforward and efficient.

CHAPTER 12

Recurrent Neural Networks (RNNs) for Sequential Data

Introduction to Recurrent Neural Networks (RNNs)

Recurrent Neural Networks (RNNs) are a class of neural networks designed specifically to work with **sequential data**. Unlike traditional feedforward neural networks, RNNs have connections that form cycles, allowing information to persist. This unique architecture allows RNNs to effectively capture **temporal dependencies** in sequential data, making them ideal for tasks such as time-series forecasting, speech recognition, language modeling, and more.

The key feature of RNNs is their ability to maintain a **memory** of previous inputs through **hidden states**, enabling them to process sequential information in a way that traditional networks cannot.

Use Cases of RNNs:

- **Time-Series Forecasting**: Predicting future values based on past data, such as stock prices or weather patterns.
- **Natural Language Processing (NLP)**: Tasks like language translation, text generation, and speech recognition.
- **Speech to Text**: Converting spoken language into written text.

Key Concepts: Hidden States, Vanishing Gradients, and LSTMs

1. **Hidden States**:
   - In an RNN, the hidden state is a vector that contains the information from previous time steps. As the network processes each element in the sequence, the hidden state is updated, carrying the relevant information from the past to the next time step.
   - This allows RNNs to "remember" previous inputs, which is important for tasks like predicting the next word in a sentence or forecasting the next value in a time-series.

Mathematically, the hidden state at time step t is updated as follows:

$$h_t = f(W_h h_{t-1} + W_x x_t + b) \quad h\_t = f(W\_h \ h\_\{t-1\} + W\_x \ x\_t + b) \quad h_t = f(W_h h_{t-1} + W_x x_t + b)$$

Where:

   - h_t h_t is the hidden state at time step t.
   - W_h W_h W_h and W_x W_x W_x are weight matrices for the hidden state and input, respectively.
   - x_t x_t is the input at time step t.
   - b b is the bias term.
2. **Vanishing Gradients**:

- One of the major challenges with traditional RNNs is the **vanishing gradient problem**. During backpropagation, when the gradients are propagated back through many time steps, they can shrink exponentially, making it difficult for the network to learn long-range dependencies in the data.
- This is a major limitation when dealing with long sequences, such as long sentences or long time-series data.

3. **Long Short-Term Memory (LSTM)**:
   - **LSTMs** are a specialized type of RNN designed to address the vanishing gradient problem. They are equipped with **gates** that control the flow of information through the network, allowing it to retain relevant information for long periods of time.
   - LSTMs consist of three main gates:
     - **Forget Gate**: Decides which information should be discarded from the cell state.
     - **Input Gate**: Updates the cell state with new information.
     - **Output Gate**: Determines the output based on the cell state.

LSTMs are widely used because they can handle long-range dependencies and are less susceptible to vanishing gradients.

Using RNNs for Time-Series Forecasting

Time-series forecasting involves predicting future values based on past observations. For example, forecasting stock prices, weather, or energy consumption.

RNNs are particularly well-suited for this task because they are capable of learning from the temporal dependencies in the data.

Steps for Time-Series Forecasting with RNNs:

1. **Prepare the Data**: Time-series data is typically structured as sequences of observations over time. We need to prepare the data for training, which often involves:
   o Reshaping the data to ensure each time step is treated as a sequence.
   o Normalizing the data to make training more efficient.
2. **Build the RNN Model**:
   o We can use an RNN or LSTM to learn from the past data and predict future values.
   o The model architecture typically includes one or more RNN/LSTM layers followed by a fully connected layer for making predictions.
3. **Train the Model**: The model is trained to minimize the loss function, often **Mean Squared Error (MSE)** for regression tasks, by adjusting the weights through backpropagation.

4. **Evaluate the Model**: We evaluate the model using a test set and assess its performance on unseen data.

Real-World Example: Stock Price Prediction with RNNs

Let's build a **Recurrent Neural Network (RNN)** for predicting **stock prices** using historical data. We'll use **LSTMs** to address the vanishing gradient problem and ensure that the model can learn from long-term dependencies in the data.

1. **Import Necessary Libraries**:

python

```python
import numpy as np
import pandas as pd
import matplotlib.pyplot as plt
from sklearn.preprocessing import MinMaxScaler
from tensorflow.keras.models import Sequential
from tensorflow.keras.layers import LSTM, Dense, Dropout
```

2. **Load and Preprocess the Stock Price Data**:

Assume we have stock price data in a CSV file. We'll load the data, normalize it, and prepare it for training.

python

```python
# Load the stock price dataset (e.g.,
historical prices of a stock)
data                            =
pd.read_csv('stock_prices.csv',
date_parser=True)
data = data[['Date', 'Close']]   #
Focus on the 'Close' price

# Normalize the data to be between 0
and 1
scaler                          =
MinMaxScaler(feature_range=(0, 1))
data_scaled                     =
scaler.fit_transform(data[['Close']]
)

# Define a function to prepare the
data for RNN training
def               prepare_data(data,
time_steps=60):
    X, y = [], []
    for   i   in   range(time_steps,
len(data)):
        X.append(data[i-
time_steps:i,  0])    #   Use   past
'time_steps' values as input
        y.append(data[i,  0])      #
Predict the next value (closing price)
    return np.array(X), np.array(y)

# Prepare the data for training
X, y = prepare_data(data_scaled)
```

```
# Reshape the input data to be 3D
(samples, time_steps, features)
X      =      X.reshape((X.shape[0],
X.shape[1], 1))
```

3. **Build the RNN Model**:

We'll use an **LSTM** layer to handle the temporal dependencies in the stock price data.

```
python
```

```
# Build the RNN model with LSTM layers
model = Sequential()

# LSTM layer with 50 units and return
sequences for the next LSTM layer
model.add(LSTM(units=50,
return_sequences=True,
input_shape=(X.shape[1], 1)))

# Dropout layer to prevent overfitting
model.add(Dropout(0.2))

# Another LSTM layer
model.add(LSTM(units=50,
return_sequences=False))

# Dropout layer
model.add(Dropout(0.2))

# Fully connected layer to output the
prediction
model.add(Dense(units=1))
```

```
# Compile the model
model.compile(optimizer='adam',
loss='mean_squared_error')
```

4. **Train the Model**:

We'll train the model using the training data, which consists of historical stock prices.

```
python
```

```
# Train the model
model.fit(X,        y,        epochs=10,
batch_size=32)
```

5. **Make Predictions**:

We can now use the trained model to predict future stock prices. We will also need to inverse transform the predictions to get them back to the original scale.

```
python
```

```
# Predict future prices using the
model
predictions = model.predict(X)

# Inverse transform the predictions to
the original scale
predictions                        =
scaler.inverse_transform(predictions
)
```

```
# Plot the results
plt.plot(data['Date'],
scaler.inverse_transform(data_scaled
), label='Actual Stock Price')
plt.plot(data['Date'][60:],
predictions, label='Predicted Stock
Price')
plt.legend()
plt.show()
```

Summary

In this chapter, we explored **Recurrent Neural Networks (RNNs)**, focusing on their suitability for **sequential data** such as time-series data. We discussed key concepts like **hidden states**, **vanishing gradients**, and **Long Short-Term Memory (LSTM)** networks, which address the challenges of training RNNs on long sequences.

We also demonstrated how to build a simple **RNN model** using **LSTMs** for **stock price prediction** with Keras and TensorFlow. By preparing the data, defining the model architecture, training it, and evaluating its performance, we showed how RNNs can be applied to real-world forecasting problems.

CHAPTER SUMMARY:

- RNNs are ideal for sequential data and can learn patterns across time.

- **LSTMs** help solve the vanishing gradient problem, enabling the network to capture long-term dependencies.
- Time-series forecasting, such as stock price prediction, is a typical application of RNNs.

CHAPTER 13

Natural Language Processing (NLP) with Python

What is NLP and Why is it Important?

Natural Language Processing (NLP) is a branch of artificial intelligence (AI) that focuses on the interaction between computers and human languages. The ultimate goal of NLP is to enable computers to understand, interpret, and generate human language in a way that is both meaningful and useful.

NLP is important because:

- **Understanding Human Language**: It allows computers to process and analyze large amounts of natural language data, helping in tasks such as information retrieval, language translation, and content recommendation.
- **Communication with Machines**: NLP is used in applications like voice assistants (e.g., Siri, Alexa), chatbots, and automated customer support systems.
- **Text Analysis**: It is also crucial for text classification, sentiment analysis, and summarization, enabling businesses to analyze customer feedback, social media content, and more.

Examples of NLP applications:

- **Machine Translation**: Translating text from one language to another (e.g., Google Translate).
- **Sentiment Analysis**: Determining the sentiment (positive, negative, neutral) of a piece of text (e.g., analyzing customer reviews).
- **Text Summarization**: Automatically generating a summary of a given text.
- **Named Entity Recognition (NER)**: Identifying and classifying entities (e.g., names, locations, dates) in text.

Tokenization, Lemmatization, and Stemming

Preprocessing text data is a crucial step in NLP to prepare it for further analysis. Three common text preprocessing techniques are **tokenization**, **lemmatization**, and **stemming**.

1. **Tokenization**:
   - Tokenization is the process of breaking down text into smaller units, known as tokens. Tokens can be words, phrases, or characters.
   - **Word Tokenization**: Splitting text into individual words.
   - **Sentence Tokenization**: Splitting text into individual sentences.

Example:

```python
```

```
from      nltk.tokenize    import
word_tokenize

text    =    "Natural    Language
Processing is amazing!"
tokens = word_tokenize(text)
print(tokens)
```

2. **Stemming**:
   - o Stemming is the process of reducing words to their base or root form. It removes prefixes and suffixes to create a word stem.
   - o For example, "running" becomes "run" and "happily" becomes "happi".
   - o **Porter Stemming** is one of the most popular stemming algorithms.

Example:

```
python
```

```
from       nltk.stem        import
PorterStemmer

ps = PorterStemmer()
words   =   ["running",   "runner",
"ran", "easily"]
stemmed_words   =   [ps.stem(word)
for word in words]
print(stemmed_words)
```

3. **Lemmatization**:

- o Lemmatization is a more advanced technique than stemming. It reduces words to their base or dictionary form (lemma). Unlike stemming, lemmatization considers the meaning of the word.
- o For example, "better" becomes "good" and "running" becomes "run".
- o **WordNet Lemmatizer** is commonly used for lemmatization.

Example:

```python

from nltk.stem import WordNetLemmatizer

lemmatizer = WordNetLemmatizer()
words = ["running", "better", "leaves", "studies"]
lemmatized_words = [lemmatizer.lemmatize(word) for word in words]
print(lemmatized_words)
```

Building a Text Classification Model with Scikit-learn

Once the text data is preprocessed, we can use **Scikit-learn** to build a text classification model. In text classification, the goal is to assign a label or category to a given text, such as classifying emails as spam or not spam, or categorizing news articles into topics.

The general process for text classification includes:

1. **Vectorization**: Converting text into a numerical format that can be processed by machine learning models. This can be done using techniques like **TF-IDF** or **Count Vectorization**.
2. **Training a Classifier**: Using algorithms like **Logistic Regression**, **Naive Bayes**, or **SVM** to classify the text based on features.
3. **Model Evaluation**: Evaluating the model's performance using metrics like **accuracy**, **precision**, and **recall**.

Let's walk through the steps of building a simple text classification model using the **SMS Spam Collection dataset**, which classifies SMS messages as spam or ham (non-spam).

1. **Import Necessary Libraries**:

python

```
import pandas as pd
from sklearn.model_selection import
train_test_split
from sklearn.feature_extraction.text
import TfidfVectorizer
from sklearn.naive_bayes import
MultinomialNB
from sklearn.metrics import
accuracy_score, classification_report
```

2. Load and Preprocess the Data:

python

```
# Load the dataset (assuming it's a
CSV file with columns 'label' and
'message')
data      =      pd.read_csv('spam.csv',
encoding='latin-1')

# Select relevant columns (label and
message)
data = data[['v1', 'v2']]
data.columns = ['label', 'message']

# Encode labels (spam = 1, ham = 0)
data['label']                          =
data['label'].map({'spam': 1, 'ham':
0})
```

3. Split the Data into Training and Test Sets:

python

```
# Split data into training and testing
sets
X_train, X_test, y_train, y_test =
train_test_split(data['message'],
data['label'],      test_size=0.2,
random_state=42)
```

4. Vectorize the Text Data:

We'll use **TF-IDF Vectorization** to convert the text messages into numerical features.

python

```
# Initialize the TF-IDF Vectorizer
vectorizer               =
TfidfVectorizer(stop_words='english'
)

# Fit and transform the training data
X_train_tfidf            =
vectorizer.fit_transform(X_train)

# Transform the test data
X_test_tfidf             =
vectorizer.transform(X_test)
```

5. Train the Classifier:

We'll use **Naive Bayes** as the classification algorithm. This is often effective for text classification tasks.

python

```
# Initialize the Naive Bayes
classifier
classifier = MultinomialNB()

# Train the model
classifier.fit(X_train_tfidf,
y_train)
```

6. Evaluate the Model:

After training the model, we can evaluate its performance on the test set.

```python
# Make predictions on the test set
y_pred = classifier.predict(X_test_tfidf)

# Evaluate the model
accuracy = accuracy_score(y_test, y_pred)
print(f"Accuracy: {accuracy}")
print(f"Classification Report:\n{classification_report(y_test, y_pred)}")
```

Real-World Example: Sentiment Analysis of Product Reviews

Sentiment Analysis is a common NLP task where the goal is to determine whether the sentiment of a piece of text is positive, negative, or neutral. In this example, we will use sentiment analysis to classify product reviews as positive or negative.

1. Load and Preprocess the Review Data:

We will assume the dataset consists of two columns: `Review` (the text of the review) and `Sentiment` (the sentiment label: Positive or Negative).

```python
```

```
# Load the dataset
reviews_data                    =
pd.read_csv('product_reviews.csv')

# Preprocess the data (convert text to
lowercase, remove stopwords, etc.)
reviews_data['Review']          =
reviews_data['Review'].str.lower()
```

2. Vectorize the Review Text:

Using **TF-IDF** vectorization, we can convert the text data into numerical features.

python

```
# Vectorize the reviews
vectorizer                      =
TfidfVectorizer(stop_words='english'
)
X                               =
vectorizer.fit_transform(reviews_dat
a['Review'])
y                               =
reviews_data['Sentiment'].map({'Posi
tive': 1, 'Negative': 0})
```

3. Train the Model:

We'll use **Logistic Regression** for sentiment classification.

python

132

```
from    sklearn.linear_model    import
LogisticRegression

# Initialize and train the Logistic
Regression model
classifier = LogisticRegression()
classifier.fit(X, y)
```

4. **Make Predictions**:

Now, we can use the trained model to predict the sentiment of new product reviews.

```
python
```

```
# Predict sentiment for a new review
new_review   =   ["This   product   is
amazing!"]
new_review_tfidf                   =
vectorizer.transform(new_review)
prediction                         =
classifier.predict(new_review_tfidf)

if prediction == 1:
    print("Positive Sentiment")
else:
    print("Negative Sentiment")
```

Summary

In this chapter, we introduced **Natural Language Processing (NLP)** and its importance in enabling machines to understand human language. We covered

133

key preprocessing techniques such as **tokenization, stemming**, and **lemmatization**, which are essential for preparing text data for machine learning models.

We then built a **text classification model** using **Scikit-learn** and the **Naive Bayes classifier**, applying it to a dataset of SMS messages for spam detection. Lastly, we walked through a real-world example of **sentiment analysis**, classifying product reviews as positive or negative.

CHAPTER SUMMARY:

- NLP enables computers to process and understand human language for a variety of applications.
- Preprocessing text data (e.g., tokenization, stemming, lemmatization) is crucial for building effective NLP models.
- **Scikit-learn** provides easy-to-use tools for text classification, and models like **Naive Bayes** are well-suited for text classification tasks.

CHAPTER 14

Working with Text Data in Python

Introduction to Text Preprocessing Techniques

Text data comes in raw form, such as plain text or HTML, and requires cleaning and transformation to make it suitable for machine learning models. **Text preprocessing** is crucial because it allows models to better understand and learn from text data.

Common preprocessing techniques include:

- **Lowercasing**: Converting all text to lowercase to ensure uniformity.
- **Removing punctuation and special characters**: Removing unnecessary characters that do not add value to text analysis.
- **Removing stopwords**: Words like "the", "a", "an", "in", and "on" that are frequent but do not carry meaningful information for NLP tasks.
- **Tokenization**: Splitting text into smaller components, usually words or sentences.
- **Stemming and Lemmatization**: Reducing words to their base or root forms.

Using Regular Expressions and Python Libraries for Text Processing

Python provides several libraries and tools to facilitate text processing. Two of the most popular libraries for text manipulation are **re** (regular expressions) and **nltk** (Natural Language Toolkit).

1. **Regular Expressions (re)**:
   o Regular expressions (regex) are sequences of characters that form search patterns. They are used for matching strings in text, finding patterns, and replacing parts of text.
   o Common tasks in text processing that use regex include:
      ▪ Removing unwanted characters or patterns (e.g., punctuation, numbers, special symbols).
      ▪ Finding specific patterns (e.g., email addresses, URLs).
      ▪ Tokenizing text into words or sentences.

Example of using **regular expressions** to remove punctuation:

```python
import re

text = "Hello! How are you doing today? Let's learn NLP."
cleaned_text = re.sub(r'[^\w\s]', '', text) # Remove punctuation
print(cleaned_text)
```

2. **NLTK (Natural Language Toolkit)**:
   - o NLTK is a powerful library for working with human language data. It provides tools for tokenization, stopword removal, stemming, lemmatization, and more.
   - o NLTK's **word_tokenize** function can be used to break text into individual words.

Example of tokenizing text with NLTK:

```python
from nltk.tokenize import word_tokenize

text = "This is a sample sentence for tokenization."
tokens = word_tokenize(text)
print(tokens)
```

Feature Extraction: Bag of Words, TF-IDF

Feature extraction is the process of converting text data into a numerical format that machine learning models can understand. Two popular methods of feature extraction are **Bag of Words** and **TF-IDF**.

1. **Bag of Words (BoW)**:
   - o The Bag of Words model represents text as an unordered collection of words, where each word's frequency is counted. It doesn't consider the grammar or word order but focuses solely on the occurrence of words.

o The result is a sparse matrix where each row represents a document and each column represents a unique word in the entire corpus.

Example:

```python
python

from sklearn.feature_extraction.text import CountVectorizer

# Sample text data
documents = ["I love machine learning", "Machine learning is fun"]

# Initialize the CountVectorizer
vectorizer = CountVectorizer()

# Fit and transform the documents
X = vectorizer.fit_transform(documents)

# Convert the result to an array and print
print(X.toarray())
print(vectorizer.get_feature_names_out())
```

2. TF-IDF (Term Frequency-Inverse Document Frequency):

- o TF-IDF is a more advanced version of BoW that adjusts the word frequency by how commonly the word appears across all documents. It helps reduce the influence of commonly occurring words (e.g., "the", "is") that are less important.
- o **Term Frequency (TF)** is the frequency of a word in a document.
- o **Inverse Document Frequency (IDF)** is a measure of how much information the word provides by considering how often it appears across all documents.

Example:

```python

from sklearn.feature_extraction.text import TfidfVectorizer

# Sample text data
documents = ["I love machine learning", "Machine learning is fun"]

# Initialize the TfidfVectorizer
tfidf_vectorizer = TfidfVectorizer()

# Fit and transform the documents
```

```
X_tfidf                    =
tfidf_vectorizer.fit_transform(d
ocuments)

# Convert the result to an array
and print
print(X_tfidf.toarray())
print(tfidf_vectorizer.get_featu
re_names_out())
```

TF-IDF is often preferred over BoW for text classification, as it considers word importance in the context of the entire dataset.

Real-World Example: Building a Spam Detector with NLP

Let's build a **spam detector** using NLP techniques. We'll use the **SMS Spam Collection dataset**, which contains labeled SMS messages (spam or ham). The goal is to classify whether a given SMS message is spam or not.

1. **Load and Preprocess the Data**:

```python

import pandas as pd

# Load the dataset
data    =    pd.read_csv('spam.csv',
encoding='latin-1')
```

```python
# Select relevant columns and rename
them
data = data[['v1', 'v2']]
data.columns = ['label', 'message']

# Encode the labels (spam = 1, ham =
0)
data['label']                        =
data['label'].map({'spam': 1, 'ham':
0})

# Sample data preview
print(data.head())
```

2. **Preprocess the Text Data**:

- Tokenize the text and remove stopwords, punctuation, and perform lemmatization.

python

```python
from       nltk.tokenize       import
word_tokenize
from nltk.corpus import stopwords
from       nltk.stem       import
WordNetLemmatizer
import re

# Initialize  the  lemmatizer  and
stopwords
lemmatizer = WordNetLemmatizer()
stop_words                        =
set(stopwords.words('english'))
```

```python
# Preprocessing function
def preprocess_text(text):
    # Remove punctuation
    text = re.sub(r'[^\w\s]', '',
text.lower())  # Convert to lowercase
and remove punctuation
    # Tokenize the text
    tokens = word_tokenize(text)
    # Remove stopwords and lemmatize
    tokens =
[lemmatizer.lemmatize(word) for word
in tokens if word not in stop_words]
    return ' '.join(tokens)

# Apply the preprocessing to each
message
data['processed_message'] =
data['message'].apply(preprocess_tex
t)

# Sample processed data
print(data[['label',
'processed_message']].head())
```

3. Feature Extraction (TF-IDF):

We will use **TF-IDF** to convert the text into numerical features.

python

```python
from sklearn.feature_extraction.text
import TfidfVectorizer
```

```
# Initialize the TfidfVectorizer
tfidf_vectorizer = TfidfVectorizer()

# Fit and transform the processed
messages
X                                   =
tfidf_vectorizer.fit_transform(data[
'processed_message'])

# Labels
y = data['label']
```

4. Split the Data into Training and Test Sets:

```
python
```

```
from sklearn.model_selection import
train_test_split

# Split the data into training and
testing sets
X_train, X_test, y_train, y_test =
train_test_split(X, y, test_size=0.2,
random_state=42)
```

5. Train the Model:

We'll use **Logistic Regression** to classify the messages as spam or ham.

```
python
```

```
from sklearn.linear_model import
LogisticRegression
```

```
# Initialize and train the model
model = LogisticRegression()
model.fit(X_train, y_train)
```

6. **Evaluate the Model**:

After training, we can evaluate the model's performance on the test data.

```
python

from       sklearn.metrics       import
accuracy_score, classification_report

# Make predictions
y_pred = model.predict(X_test)

# Evaluate the model
accuracy   =   accuracy_score(y_test,
y_pred)
print(f"Accuracy: {accuracy}")
print(f"Classification
Report:\n{classification_report(y_te
st, y_pred)}")
```

Summary

In this chapter, we learned how to work with **text data** in Python, covering important preprocessing techniques like **tokenization, stemming, lemmatization,** and **regular expressions**. We also explored **feature extraction** methods such as **Bag of Words** and **TF-**

IDF, which transform text data into numerical formats that machine learning models can understand.

Finally, we built a **spam detector** using NLP techniques, demonstrating how to preprocess text, extract features, and train a classification model with **Logistic Regression**.

CHAPTER SUMMARY:

- **Text preprocessing** is essential for preparing raw text data for machine learning.
- **TF-IDF** is a powerful feature extraction method for text classification.
- **Scikit-learn** makes it easy to implement and evaluate text classification models.

CHAPTER 15

Hyperparameter Tuning for Better Models

What Are Hyperparameters and Why They Matter?

In machine learning, **hyperparameters** are the parameters that are set **before** training the model and cannot be learned from the data directly. They control various aspects of the training process and have a significant impact on the performance of the model.

Examples of hyperparameters include:

- **Learning rate**: The step size at which the model updates its parameters during training. A high learning rate may lead to overshooting the optimal solution, while a low learning rate may result in slow convergence.
- **Number of hidden layers and neurons** in a neural network: The depth and width of the network affect its capacity to learn from the data.
- **Batch size**: The number of samples processed before the model's internal parameters are updated.
- **Number of trees** in a random forest or **depth of trees**.
- **Kernel** in a support vector machine (SVM): Determines the type of decision boundary (linear or non-linear).

Why Hyperparameters Matter:

- The choice of hyperparameters can drastically influence the model's **accuracy**, **training time**, and **generalization** ability. Poorly chosen hyperparameters may lead to underfitting or overfitting.
- Hyperparameter tuning is the process of searching for the best combination of hyperparameters that results in optimal performance for the model.

Techniques for Hyperparameter Tuning: Grid Search, Random Search

1. **Grid Search**:
   o **Grid Search** is a brute-force approach to hyperparameter tuning. It exhaustively searches through a specified set of hyperparameters and evaluates all possible combinations.
   o For example, if you want to tune the **learning rate** and the **batch size**, you could define a grid with multiple values for each and perform grid search to evaluate every possible combination of parameters.

   Advantages:

   o It's guaranteed to find the best combination within the grid search space.
   o Simple to implement.

   Disadvantages:

- o Computationally expensive, especially if the grid is large.
- o Not efficient when the hyperparameter search space is large.

Example of **Grid Search** in **Scikit-learn**:

python

```
from      sklearn.model_selection
import GridSearchCV
from    sklearn.ensemble    import
RandomForestClassifier

# Define the model
model = RandomForestClassifier()

# Define the hyperparameter grid
param_grid = {
    'n_estimators':   [100,   200,
300],
    'max_depth': [10, 20, 30],
    'min_samples_split':   [2,   5,
10]
}

# Initialize GridSearchCV
grid_search                    =
GridSearchCV(estimator=model,
param_grid=param_grid, cv=5)

# Fit the grid search
grid_search.fit(X_train,
y_train)
```

```
# Best parameters
print("Best parameters found: ",
grid_search.best_params_)
```

2. **Random Search**:
   - o **Random Search** randomly samples hyperparameters from the specified search space. Unlike grid search, it doesn't evaluate every combination but instead selects random combinations, making it more efficient when the search space is large.

Advantages:

   - o More computationally efficient than grid search.
   - o Works well when only a few hyperparameters significantly impact the model's performance.

Disadvantages:

   - o It may not find the best combination if the search space is large.

Example of **Random Search** in **Scikit-learn**:

```python
from       sklearn.model_selection
import RandomizedSearchCV
```

```python
from    sklearn.ensemble    import
RandomForestClassifier
from scipy.stats import randint

# Define the model
model = RandomForestClassifier()

#    Define    the    hyperparameter
distribution
param_dist = {
    'n_estimators': randint(100,
1000),
    'max_depth':       randint(10,
50),
    'min_samples_split':
randint(2, 10)
}

# Initialize RandomizedSearchCV
random_search                 =
RandomizedSearchCV(estimator=mod
el,
param_distributions=param_dist,
n_iter=100, cv=5)

# Fit the random search
random_search.fit(X_train,
y_train)

# Best parameters
print("Best parameters found: ",
random_search.best_params_)
```

Cross-Validation for Better Model Generalization

Cross-validation is a technique used to assess the generalization performance of a machine learning model. It splits the dataset into multiple subsets (folds) and trains the model multiple times, each time using a different fold for validation and the remaining data for training. The goal of cross-validation is to provide a better estimate of the model's performance on unseen data and to reduce the impact of overfitting.

Common types of cross-validation:

- **K-Fold Cross-Validation**: The data is split into kkk subsets (or folds), and the model is trained kkk times, each time using one fold as the validation set and the remaining k−1k-1k−1 folds for training.
- **Stratified K-Fold Cross-Validation**: Similar to k-fold, but ensures that each fold has the same proportion of class labels (useful for imbalanced datasets).
- **Leave-One-Out Cross-Validation (LOOCV)**: A special case of k-fold cross-validation where kkk equals the total number of data points. This means each data point gets its turn as the validation set.

Example of **K-Fold Cross-Validation** in **Scikit-learn**:

python

```python
from sklearn.model_selection import
cross_val_score
from      sklearn.ensemble      import
RandomForestClassifier

# Define the model
model = RandomForestClassifier()

# Perform 5-fold cross-validation
cv_scores = cross_val_score(model,
X_train, y_train, cv=5)

# Print the cross-validation scores
print(f"Cross-validation      scores:
{cv_scores}")
print(f"Mean cross-validation score:
{cv_scores.mean()}")
```

Why Cross-Validation is Important:

- It provides a more reliable estimate of the model's performance, especially when working with small datasets.
- It helps in detecting overfitting, as the model is validated on different subsets of the data.
- It is often used alongside hyperparameter tuning to ensure that the model generalizes well across different hyperparameter choices.

Real-World Example: Improving Model Accuracy with Hyperparameter Tuning

Let's consider a real-world scenario where we are trying to build a **Random Forest model** to predict customer churn, and we want to improve the model's accuracy using **hyperparameter tuning**.

1. **Load and Preprocess the Data**:

python

```
import pandas as pd
from sklearn.model_selection import
train_test_split

# Load the customer churn dataset
data                            =
pd.read_csv('customer_churn.csv')

# Select features and target
X = data.drop('Churn', axis=1)
y = data['Churn']

# Split the data into training and
testing sets
X_train, X_test, y_train, y_test =
train_test_split(X, y, test_size=0.2,
random_state=42)
```

2. **Use Grid Search or Random Search for Hyperparameter Tuning**:

We'll use **Grid Search** to find the optimal number of trees and maximum depth for the Random Forest classifier.

python

```python
from sklearn.ensemble import RandomForestClassifier
from sklearn.model_selection import GridSearchCV

# Initialize the model
model = RandomForestClassifier(random_state=42)

# Define the hyperparameter grid
param_grid = {
    'n_estimators': [100, 200, 300],
    'max_depth': [10, 20, 30],
    'min_samples_split': [2, 5, 10]
}

# Initialize GridSearchCV
grid_search = GridSearchCV(estimator=model, param_grid=param_grid, cv=5)

# Fit the grid search to the training data
grid_search.fit(X_train, y_train)

# Best parameters
```

```
print("Best    parameters    found:    ",
grid_search.best_params_)
```

3. **Evaluate the Model**:

Once we've found the best hyperparameters, we can evaluate the model's performance on the test data.

```
python
```

```python
# Best model from GridSearchCV
best_model                          =
grid_search.best_estimator_

# Evaluate on test data
test_accuracy                       =
best_model.score(X_test, y_test)
print(f"Test                Accuracy:
{test_accuracy}")
```

4. **Improve the Model's Accuracy**:

By using hyperparameter tuning, we can improve the model's performance. Hyperparameter tuning ensures that the model is configured to learn the most relevant features from the data, which ultimately leads to higher accuracy.

Summary

In this chapter, we learned about **hyperparameter tuning**, which is crucial for improving the performance of machine learning models. We discussed the importance of **hyperparameters**, common techniques like **Grid Search** and **Random Search**, and how **cross-validation** helps assess model performance more reliably. We also walked through a real-world example of using **hyperparameter tuning** to improve the accuracy of a **Random Forest** model for customer churn prediction.

CHAPTER SUMMARY:

- Hyperparameters play a crucial role in determining a model's performance, and their tuning can significantly improve results.
- **Grid Search** and **Random Search** are effective techniques for finding the best hyperparameters, with Grid Search being exhaustive and Random Search being more efficient for larger search spaces.
- **Cross-validation** is essential for assessing the generalization of the model and preventing overfitting.

CHAPTER 16

Introduction to Reinforcement Learning

What is Reinforcement Learning and How is It Different from Supervised/Unsupervised Learning?

Reinforcement Learning (RL) is a type of machine learning where an agent learns to make decisions by interacting with an environment. The agent receives feedback in the form of **rewards** or **penalties** based on the actions it takes and aims to maximize the cumulative reward over time. Unlike **supervised** or **unsupervised learning**, where the learning process is guided by labeled data or patterns in the data, RL is based on trial and error, and the agent learns from the consequences of its actions.

1. **Supervised Learning**:
   - In supervised learning, the model learns from a labeled dataset where the correct output (target) is provided for each input. The goal is to learn a mapping from inputs to outputs.
   - Example: Classifying emails as spam or not spam, where the label is provided.
2. **Unsupervised Learning**:
   - In unsupervised learning, the model learns from data without labels. The goal is to discover patterns, groupings, or structures in the data.
   - Example: Clustering customers based on purchasing behavior.

3. **Reinforcement Learning**:
   - o In RL, the agent interacts with an environment and learns through **feedback** in the form of rewards or penalties. The agent aims to take actions that maximize the long-term reward, rather than just learning from labeled data.
   - o Example: Training a robot to walk or teaching a self-driving car how to drive by rewarding correct driving decisions.

Key Differences:

- **Supervised Learning**: Learns from labeled data (input-output pairs).
- **Unsupervised Learning**: Learns patterns from unlabeled data.
- **Reinforcement Learning**: Learns through interaction with the environment and receives feedback in the form of rewards or penalties.

Key Concepts: Agents, Actions, Rewards

1. **Agent**:
   - o The agent is the decision-maker in reinforcement learning. It interacts with the environment by taking actions and observing the resulting states and rewards.
   - o The goal of the agent is to learn a **policy**, which is a strategy for deciding which action to take at any given state.
2. **Actions**:

- o Actions are the moves or decisions that the agent can take in the environment. In each state, the agent has a set of possible actions to choose from.
- o The quality of the action is determined by the **reward** it generates.

3. **Rewards**:
   - o A reward is the feedback the agent receives after taking an action. It is a scalar value that signals how good or bad an action was in achieving the agent's goal.
   - o **Positive rewards** encourage the agent to repeat the action, while **negative rewards** (penalties) discourage the action.
   - o The agent's objective is to maximize the cumulative reward over time, often referred to as **return**.

4. **State**:
   - o The state represents the current situation of the environment. The agent uses the state to determine which action to take.
   - o For example, in a game, the state could be the current position of the player, the health level, and the score.

Real-World Example: Building a Q-Learning Agent to Navigate a Maze

One of the simplest and most popular algorithms in reinforcement learning is **Q-learning**. Q-learning is a model-free algorithm that allows an agent to learn how to act optimally in a given environment by learning the value of state-action pairs (called Q-values).

The key idea behind Q-learning is that the agent learns the expected utility (Q-value) of performing an action in a particular state and updates these values over time using the reward feedback.

Let's build a **Q-learning agent** that learns how to navigate a simple maze. The agent starts at a position in the maze and must learn to navigate towards the goal (reward) while avoiding obstacles.

1. **Defining the Environment**:

We'll define a simple grid maze where the agent has to navigate from a starting point to a goal.

```python
import numpy as np

# Define the grid size
grid_size = (5, 5)

# Define the maze environment
# 0 - Empty space
# 1 - Wall (Obstacle)
# 2 - Goal
maze = np.array([
    [0, 0, 0, 0, 0],
    [0, 1, 1, 0, 0],
    [0, 1, 0, 0, 0],
    [0, 1, 0, 1, 0],
```

```
    [0, 0, 0, 0, 2]
])
```

```
# Define the start and goal positions
start = (0, 0)
goal = (4, 4)
```

```
# Define possible actions: up, down,
left, right
actions = ['up', 'down', 'left',
'right']
```

2. Q-Learning Setup:

We will initialize the Q-table, which stores the Q-values for each state-action pair. Initially, all Q-values are set to zero.

```
python
```

```
# Initialize the Q-table
Q      =      np.zeros((grid_size[0],
grid_size[1], len(actions)))
```

```
# Define parameters
alpha = 0.1   # Learning rate
gamma = 0.9   # Discount factor
epsilon = 0.2 # Exploration factor
```

3. Defining the Reward Function:

- The reward function is defined as follows:
    - +1 for reaching the goal.
    - -1 for hitting a wall.

- -**0.01** for each step taken (to encourage the agent to find the shortest path).

python

```python
def reward_function(state, action):
    # Check if the action leads to a valid state
    x, y = state
    if action == 'up' and x > 0: x -= 1
    elif action == 'down' and x < grid_size[0] - 1: x += 1
    elif action == 'left' and y > 0: y -= 1
    elif action == 'right' and y < grid_size[1] - 1: y += 1

    # Check if the new position is the goal
    if (x, y) == goal:
        return 1
    elif maze[x, y] == 1:    # Hit a wall
        return -1
    else:  # Empty space
        return -0.01
```

4. **Q-Learning Algorithm**:

The agent learns through exploration and exploitation. The exploration allows the agent to try different actions, while exploitation enables it to select the best action based on the current Q-values.

```python
python

def q_learning(episodes=1000):
    for episode in range(episodes):
        state = start  # Start at the beginning of each episode
        done = False

        while not done:
            # Choose action based on epsilon-greedy strategy
            if np.random.rand() < epsilon:
                action = np.random.choice(actions)        # Exploration
            else:
                action = actions[np.argmax(Q[state[0], state[1]])]  # Exploitation

            # Get the reward for the action
            reward = reward_function(state, action)

            # Find the new state
            x, y = state
            if action == 'up' and x > 0: x -= 1
            elif action == 'down' and x < grid_size[0] - 1: x += 1
```

```
        elif action == 'left' and
y > 0: y -= 1
        elif  action  ==  'right'
and y < grid_size[1] - 1: y += 1
        new_state = (x, y)

        # Update Q-value using
the Q-learning formula
        Q[state[0],    state[1],
actions.index(action)] = Q[state[0],
state[1], actions.index(action)] + \
        alpha * (reward +
gamma  *  np.max(Q[new_state[0],
new_state[1]])     -     Q[state[0],
state[1], actions.index(action)])

        # If the agent reaches the
goal, end the episode
        if new_state == goal:
            done = True

        # Update the state
        state = new_state

q_learning()
```

5. **Visualizing the Learned Path**:

After the Q-learning agent has learned the optimal policy, we can visualize the path it would take to reach the goal.

```
python
```

```python
def visualize_path():
    state = start
    path = [state]
    while state != goal:
        action                   = actions[np.argmax(Q[state[0], state[1]])]
        print(f"Current       state: {state}, Action: {action}")

        # Move according to the best action
        x, y = state
        if action == 'up' and x > 0: x -= 1
        elif action == 'down' and x < grid_size[0] - 1: x += 1
        elif action == 'left' and y > 0: y -= 1
        elif action == 'right' and y < grid_size[1] - 1: y += 1
        state = (x, y)

        path.append(state)

    print(f"Optimal path: {path}")

# Visualize the learned path
visualize_path()
```

165

Summary

In this chapter, we introduced **Reinforcement Learning (RL)**, highlighting the key differences between RL and other machine learning paradigms like **supervised** and **unsupervised learning**. We explored the core components of RL, including **agents**, **actions**, and **rewards**, and discussed the fundamental Q-learning algorithm.

We also demonstrated a **Q-learning agent** that learns to navigate a maze. The agent explores different actions and learns the optimal path by maximizing rewards using the Q-learning algorithm.

CHAPTER SUMMARY:

- **Reinforcement Learning** enables an agent to learn through interaction with its environment, receiving feedback in the form of rewards or penalties.
- **Q-learning** is a simple yet powerful RL algorithm used to find the optimal policy for an agent by learning Q-values for state-action pairs.
- RL is applicable in various domains, including robotics, gaming, and autonomous systems.

CHAPTER 17

Feature Engineering for Machine Learning

The Importance of Features in Machine Learning Models

In machine learning, **features** are the input variables or attributes that represent the data. The performance of a machine learning model heavily depends on the quality of the features it uses. Good features allow the model to capture relevant patterns in the data and make accurate predictions, while poor features can lead to underfitting or overfitting.

Why Features Matter:

1. **Improving Model Accuracy**: Well-engineered features can significantly improve the predictive power of a model.
2. **Reducing Complexity**: Selecting or transforming features can reduce the dimensionality of the dataset, making the model simpler and faster to train.
3. **Handling Different Data Types**: Machine learning models require numerical input, so feature engineering is often necessary to convert categorical, text, and image data into a usable format.
4. **Domain Knowledge**: Feature engineering often involves applying domain knowledge to create meaningful variables that enhance the model's ability to learn.

167

Techniques for Feature Extraction and Transformation

Feature extraction and transformation are crucial steps in the machine learning pipeline. These techniques help create useful features from raw data and improve the model's ability to learn meaningful patterns.

1. **Scaling and Normalization**:
   - **Scaling**: This process transforms features to a common scale, typically between 0 and 1. This is especially important for algorithms that rely on distance metrics (e.g., K-Nearest Neighbors, SVMs).
   - **Normalization**: This is a specific case of scaling, where the data is scaled to have a mean of 0 and a standard deviation of 1. It is commonly used in neural networks.

Example (Min-Max Scaling):

```python
from        sklearn.preprocessing
import MinMaxScaler

scaler = MinMaxScaler()
scaled_data                      =
scaler.fit_transform(data[['feat
ure1', 'feature2']])
```

2. **One-Hot Encoding**:
   - One-hot encoding is a technique for converting categorical variables into

binary vectors, where each category is represented by a unique vector. This allows machine learning algorithms to work with categorical data.

o For example, if a feature "Color" has values "Red", "Green", and "Blue", one-hot encoding would create three binary columns, one for each color.

Example:

python

```
from         sklearn.preprocessing
import OneHotEncoder

encoder = OneHotEncoder()
encoded_data                    =
encoder.fit_transform(data[['Col
or']])
```

3. **Binning**:
   o Binning is a technique used to group continuous features into discrete bins or categories. This is useful for features that have a non-linear relationship with the target variable. For example, ages can be grouped into age ranges (e.g., 18-25, 26-35, etc.).

Example:

python

```
import pandas as pd

bins = [0, 18, 25, 35, 50, 100]
labels = ['0-18', '19-25', '26-
35', '36-50', '51+']
data['Age_Binned']            =
pd.cut(data['Age'],     bins=bins,
labels=labels)
```

4. **Polynomial Features**:
   - Polynomial features are created by adding higher-order terms of the original features. This technique is useful for capturing non-linear relationships in the data.
   - For example, if a feature is xxx, you can create new features like x2x^2x2, x3x^3x3, and so on.

Example:

python

```
from         sklearn.preprocessing
import PolynomialFeatures

poly                            =
PolynomialFeatures(degree=2)
poly_features                   =
poly.fit_transform(data[['featur
e1']])
```

5. **Principal Component Analysis (PCA)**:

- o PCA is a dimensionality reduction technique that transforms the original features into a smaller set of features (principal components) that capture the most variance in the data.
- o It is useful when dealing with high-dimensional datasets to improve model performance and reduce overfitting.

Example:

```python

from         sklearn.decomposition
import PCA

pca = PCA(n_components=2)
reduced_data                    =
pca.fit_transform(data[['feature
1', 'feature2', 'feature3']])
```

Handling Categorical Data and Text Features

Machine learning models require numerical input, so categorical and text data must be converted into a numerical format before they can be used.

1. **Handling Categorical Data**:
   - o **Label Encoding**: Converts each category in a feature to a unique integer. This is useful when the categorical feature has a natural ordering (e.g., "Low", "Medium", "High").

Example:

```python
python
```

```python
from        sklearn.preprocessing
import LabelEncoder

encoder = LabelEncoder()
data['encoded_column']         =
encoder.fit_transform(data['cate
gorical_column'])
```

- o **One-Hot Encoding**: As mentioned earlier, one-hot encoding is used for unordered categorical data. It creates a binary column for each category in the original feature.
2. **Handling Text Features**:
   - o **Bag of Words (BoW)**: A method to convert text into a numerical format. It represents the text as a matrix where each column represents a unique word from the corpus, and the value represents the frequency of that word in the document.

Example:

```python
python
```

```python
from
sklearn.feature_extraction.text
import CountVectorizer
```

```
vectorizer = CountVectorizer()
X                            =
vectorizer.fit_transform(data['t
ext_column'])
```

  o **TF-IDF (Term Frequency-Inverse Document Frequency)**: As mentioned in Chapter 14, TF-IDF is a more advanced technique than BoW that considers the frequency of words in individual documents and the entire corpus, which helps reduce the weight of commonly occurring words.

Example:

```
python

from
sklearn.feature_extraction.text
import TfidfVectorizer

tfidf_vectorizer              =
TfidfVectorizer()
X_tfidf                       =
tfidf_vectorizer.fit_transform(d
ata['text_column'])
```

3. **Word Embeddings**:
  o Word embeddings, such as **Word2Vec** or **GloVe**, convert words into continuous vectors of fixed size, capturing semantic relationships between words. These are

especially useful for deep learning models that process text data.

o Word embeddings allow similar words to have similar vector representations (e.g., "king" and "queen" would have similar vectors).

Example (using **Gensim** for Word2Vec):

python

```
from       gensim.models       import
Word2Vec

sentences = [['this', 'is', 'a',
'sentence'],           ['another',
'sentence']]
model     =     Word2Vec(sentences,
min_count=1)
vector = model.wv['sentence']
print(vector)
```

Real-World Example: Preparing Features for a Predictive Model

Let's build a simple **predictive model** for predicting **customer churn** using feature engineering. We'll assume we have a dataset with the following features: age,   gender,   subscription_type, account_balance, and churn (target variable).

1. **Load and Explore the Data**:

python

```python
import pandas as pd

# Load the dataset
data                                    =
pd.read_csv('customer_churn.csv')

# Preview the data
print(data.head())
```

2. **Handle Missing Values**:

```
python
```

```python
# Fill missing values with the mean or
mode depending on the feature type
data['age'].fillna(data['age'].mean(
), inplace=True)
data['gender'].fillna(data['gender']
.mode()[0], inplace=True)
```

3. **Feature Engineering**:

- **Scaling Numerical Features**:

```
python
```

```python
from    sklearn.preprocessing    import
MinMaxScaler

scaler = MinMaxScaler()
data[['age',  'account_balance']]  =
scaler.fit_transform(data[['age',
'account_balance']])
```

- **One-Hot Encoding for Categorical Features**:

python

```
data          =          pd.get_dummies(data,
columns=['gender',
'subscription_type'],
drop_first=True)
```

- **Create New Features (e.g., Age Bins)**:

python

```
bins = [0, 18, 35, 50, 100]
labels = ['0-18', '19-35', '36-50',
'51+']
data['age_group']                      =
pd.cut(data['age'],         bins=bins,
labels=labels)
```

4. **Split the Data into Training and Test Sets**:

python

```
from  sklearn.model_selection  import
train_test_split

X = data.drop('churn', axis=1)    #
Features
y = data['churn']  # Target

X_train, X_test, y_train, y_test =
train_test_split(X, y, test_size=0.2,
random_state=42)
```

5. **Train the Model**:

Let's train a simple **Logistic Regression** model for customer churn prediction.

python

```
from sklearn.linear_model import LogisticRegression
from sklearn.metrics import accuracy_score, classification_report

# Train the model
model = LogisticRegression()
model.fit(X_train, y_train)

# Make predictions
y_pred = model.predict(X_test)

# Evaluate the model
print(f"Accuracy: {accuracy_score(y_test, y_pred)}")
print(classification_report(y_test, y_pred))
```

Summary

In this chapter, we explored **feature engineering**, a crucial process that enhances the performance of machine learning models by transforming raw data into useful features. We discussed various techniques for feature extraction and transformation, including scaling, one-hot encoding, text feature handling, and dimensionality reduction.

We also demonstrated how to handle **categorical data** and **text features** and applied these techniques in a **customer churn prediction model**.

CHAPTER SUMMARY:

- **Feature engineering** is essential for improving model performance and ensuring that the model can learn relevant patterns from the data.
- Techniques such as **scaling**, **one-hot encoding**, and **TF-IDF** help prepare data for machine learning algorithms.
- **Domain knowledge** is key to creating meaningful features that enhance model learning.

CHAPTER 18

Model Optimization and Regularization

Understanding Overfitting and Underfitting

In machine learning, the goal is to build a model that generalizes well to unseen data. However, models can suffer from two common problems: **overfitting** and **underfitting**.

1. **Overfitting**:
   o **Definition**: Overfitting occurs when a model learns the training data too well, including its noise and fluctuations, which leads to poor performance on new, unseen data.
   o **Signs of Overfitting**:
     ▪ High accuracy on the training set but poor performance on the test set.
     ▪ The model is too complex, with too many parameters relative to the amount of training data.
   o **Cause**: Overfitting happens when the model is too flexible, meaning it can fit the training data very closely (e.g., very deep decision trees or high-degree polynomial regression).
2. **Underfitting**:
   o **Definition**: Underfitting occurs when a model is too simple to capture the underlying patterns in the data, leading to

poor performance on both the training set and the test set.

- o **Signs of Underfitting**:
  - ▪ Poor accuracy on both the training and test sets.
  - ▪ The model is too simplistic and unable to capture complex patterns in the data (e.g., using linear regression on data that has a non-linear relationship).
- o **Cause**: Underfitting happens when the model is too rigid or not complex enough to learn the data's underlying structure (e.g., using a linear model for non-linear data).

Balancing Overfitting and Underfitting:

- The key challenge is to find the right balance. You want a model that is **complex enough** to capture meaningful patterns but **simple enough** to generalize to new data.
- **Regularization** is a technique used to prevent overfitting by adding a penalty to the model's complexity.

Techniques for Regularization: L1, L2 Regularization

Regularization involves adding a penalty term to the loss function to constrain the complexity of the model. This helps prevent overfitting by discouraging the model from relying too heavily on any particular feature.

1. **L1 Regularization (Lasso)**:
   - **Definition**: L1 regularization adds the absolute values of the model's coefficients as a penalty to the loss function. This can result in some coefficients being reduced to zero, effectively performing **feature selection**.
   - **Formula**:
     Loss=Loss Function+$\lambda \sum$i=1n|wi|\text{L oss} = \text{Loss Function} + \lambda \sum_{i=1}^{n}
     |w_i|Loss=Loss Function+λi=1$\sum$n|wi|
     Where wiw_iwi represents the weights, and λ\lambda$\lambda$ is the regularization parameter that controls the strength of the penalty.
   - **Effect**: L1 regularization encourages sparsity in the model, which can lead to a simpler, more interpretable model by eliminating less important features.
2. **L2 Regularization (Ridge)**:
   - **Definition**: L2 regularization adds the square of the model's coefficients as a penalty to the loss function. This does not set any coefficients to zero but instead shrinks them towards zero, encouraging smaller weights.
   - **Formula**:
     Loss=Loss Function+$\lambda \sum$i=1nwi2\text{L oss} = \text{Loss Function} + \lambda \sum_{i=1}^{n}
     w_i^2Loss=Loss Function+λi=1$\sum$nwi2
     Where wiw_iwi represents the weights,

and λ\lambdaλ is the regularization parameter.

- o **Effect**: L2 regularization prevents overfitting by reducing the magnitude of the coefficients, but unlike L1, it does not eliminate any features entirely.

3. **Elastic Net**:

- o Elastic Net is a hybrid of L1 and L2 regularization that combines the benefits of both methods. It allows for both sparsity (feature selection) and coefficient shrinkage.

- o The formula combines both L1 and L2 penalties:
  $$\text{Loss} = \text{Loss Function} + \lambda_1 \sum_{i=1}^{n} |w_i| + \lambda_2 \sum_{i=1}^{n} w_i^2$$

Model Selection and Cross-Validation

1. **Model Selection**:

- o Model selection involves choosing the best model from a set of candidate models based on performance metrics. This can involve comparing models with different hyperparameters, architectures, or algorithms.

- o **Bias-Variance Tradeoff**: Model selection is often driven by the tradeoff between **bias** (error due to overly simplistic models) and **variance** (error due to overly complex models).

- o **Regularization** is a key part of model selection, as it helps manage the complexity of the model.

2. **Cross-Validation**:
   - o Cross-validation is a technique used to assess the generalization performance of a model. It involves splitting the data into multiple folds and training the model on different subsets of the data, then testing it on the remaining fold. This helps reduce overfitting by ensuring that the model is evaluated on multiple data subsets.
   - o **K-Fold Cross-Validation**:
     - The dataset is split into kkk equal-sized folds. The model is trained on k−1k-1k−1 folds and tested on the remaining fold. This process is repeated kkk times, each time with a different fold as the test set.
   - o **Stratified K-Fold Cross-Validation**: This is useful for imbalanced datasets, as it ensures that each fold has a similar distribution of the target variable.

Example of **K-Fold Cross-Validation** in **Scikit-learn**:

```python
from      sklearn.model_selection
import cross_val_score
```

```
from sklearn.linear_model import
LogisticRegression

# Define the model
model = LogisticRegression()

# Perform 5-fold cross-validation
cv_scores                        =
cross_val_score(model,   X_train,
y_train,  cv=5)

# Print the results
print(f"Cross-validation scores:
{cv_scores}")
print(f"Mean        cross-validation
score: {cv_scores.mean()}")
```

*Real-World Example: Improving Model Generalization
with Regularization*

Let's work through an example where we apply
regularization to improve a **Logistic Regression**
model for predicting **customer churn**.

1. **Load and Preprocess the Data**:

```
python

import pandas as pd
from sklearn.model_selection  import
train_test_split
from  sklearn.preprocessing  import
StandardScaler
```

```python
# Load the dataset
data                          =
pd.read_csv('customer_churn.csv')

# Split the dataset into features (X)
and target (y)
X = data.drop('churn', axis=1)
y = data['churn']

# Split the data into training and
testing sets
X_train, X_test, y_train, y_test =
train_test_split(X, y, test_size=0.2,
random_state=42)

# Scale the features
scaler = StandardScaler()
X_train_scaled                =
scaler.fit_transform(X_train)
X_test_scaled                 =
scaler.transform(X_test)
```

2. **Train a Logistic Regression Model with L2 Regularization (Ridge)**:

```python
python

from    sklearn.linear_model    import
LogisticRegression
from      sklearn.metrics      import
accuracy_score

# Train a logistic regression model
with L2 regularization (Ridge)
```

```python
model                           =
LogisticRegression(penalty='l2',
C=1.0)    #  C  is  the  inverse  of
regularization strength
model.fit(X_train_scaled, y_train)

# Make predictions
y_pred = model.predict(X_test_scaled)

# Evaluate the model
accuracy    =    accuracy_score(y_test,
y_pred)
print(f"Accuracy        with        L2
regularization: {accuracy}")
```

3. **Compare with L1 Regularization (Lasso)**:

```
python
```

```python
# Train  a  logistic  regression  model
with L1 regularization (Lasso)
model_l1                         =
LogisticRegression(penalty='l1',
solver='liblinear', C=1.0)
model_l1.fit(X_train_scaled, y_train)

# Make predictions
y_pred_l1                        =
model_l1.predict(X_test_scaled)

# Evaluate the model
accuracy_l1 = accuracy_score(y_test,
y_pred_l1)
```

```
print(f"Accuracy          with          L1
regularization: {accuracy_l1}")
```

4. **Model Evaluation and Conclusion**:
   - By comparing the accuracy and performance of the models with **L1** and **L2 regularization**, we can determine which method helps reduce overfitting and improves generalization.
   - Regularization helps prevent the model from becoming too complex and overfitting the training data, improving its ability to generalize to unseen data.

Summary

In this chapter, we discussed the challenges of **overfitting** and **underfitting** in machine learning models and how **regularization** techniques like **L1** (Lasso) and **L2** (Ridge) can help mitigate overfitting by penalizing large model coefficients.

We also explored **model selection** and the importance of **cross-validation** in assessing a model's generalization ability. Through a real-world example, we demonstrated how to apply **regularization** in **Logistic Regression** to improve model accuracy and generalization for customer churn prediction.

CHAPTER SUMMARY:

- **Overfitting** and **underfitting** are common challenges, and regularization techniques help manage model complexity.
- **L1** and **L2 regularization** help prevent overfitting by adding a penalty to the loss function.
- **Cross-validation** is essential for evaluating the model's ability to generalize to new, unseen data.

CHAPTER 19

Building Your First AI Chatbot

What is an AI Chatbot and How Does It Work?

An **AI chatbot** is a computer program designed to simulate human conversation through text or voice interactions. Chatbots are often used in customer service, virtual assistants, and various other domains to automate interactions and provide users with quick responses to their queries.

How AI Chatbots Work:

1. **User Input**: The user sends a message or query to the chatbot.
2. **Natural Language Processing (NLP)**: The chatbot uses NLP techniques to understand the user's intent by processing the input text.
3. **Response Generation**: Based on the user input, the chatbot generates an appropriate response, either by following predefined rules or using machine learning models.
4. **Output**: The chatbot replies to the user with the generated response, which could be a text, a recommendation, or an action.

AI chatbots can be classified into two main types:

- **Rule-based Chatbots**: These chatbots follow predefined scripts and rules to generate responses. They are typically used for simple tasks and have a limited scope.

- **Machine Learning-based Chatbots**: These chatbots learn from large datasets and can generate more complex and dynamic responses. They use NLP techniques to understand and generate human-like responses.

Techniques for Building Rule-Based and Machine Learning-Based Chatbots

1. **Rule-Based Chatbots**:
   - **Definition**: Rule-based chatbots follow a set of predefined rules and respond to specific patterns or keywords in the user input. They do not learn from data and can only handle interactions defined by the rules.
   - **How It Works**: The chatbot uses regular expressions or simple matching techniques to detect specific keywords or patterns in the user's message and responds based on predefined rules.
   - **Advantages**: Easy to implement and deploy; ideal for handling repetitive tasks or specific queries.
   - **Disadvantages**: Limited flexibility; cannot handle complex or unforeseen user inputs.

Example:

```python
```

```
import re

def
rule_based_chatbot(user_input):
    if
re.search(r'\b(hi|hello|hey)\b',
user_input, re.I):
        return "Hello! How can I
help you today?"
    elif   re.search(r'\bbye\b',
user_input, re.I):
        return "Goodbye! Have a
great day!"
    else:
        return "Sorry, I didn't
understand   that.   Can   you
rephrase?"

# Example interaction
print(rule_based_chatbot("hi"))
print(rule_based_chatbot("bye"))
print(rule_based_chatbot("tell
me a joke"))
```

2. **Machine Learning-Based Chatbots**:
   o **Definition**: These chatbots use machine learning techniques to process and understand user inputs. They learn from large datasets and can handle a wider variety of user queries.
   o **How It Works**: Machine learning-based chatbots typically use **Natural Language**

Understanding (NLU) to extract meaning from the user input and **Natural Language Generation (NLG)** to generate appropriate responses. The model can be trained on labeled conversational data to improve its ability to generate meaningful responses.

- o **Techniques**:
  - • **Intent Recognition**: Identifying the user's intent (e.g., booking a flight, checking the weather).
  - • **Entity Recognition**: Extracting specific information from the user input (e.g., dates, locations).
- o **Advantages**: More flexible and capable of handling complex conversations.
- o **Disadvantages**: Requires large amounts of labeled training data and computational resources.

Example using a simple machine learning model with Scikit-learn:

python

```
from
sklearn.feature_extraction.text
import CountVectorizer
from sklearn.naive_bayes import
MultinomialNB

# Sample data for intent
classification
```

```python
intents = ["greet", "goodbye",
"check_weather"]
training_sentences = ["hi",
"hello", "hey", "bye", "goodbye",
"what's the weather like?",
"check the weather"]
labels = [0, 0, 0, 1, 1, 2, 2] #
Labels corresponding to the
intents

# Vectorizing the input text
vectorizer = CountVectorizer()
X =
vectorizer.fit_transform(trainin
g_sentences)

# Train the Naive Bayes
classifier
model = MultinomialNB()
model.fit(X, labels)

# Predict the intent of a user
input
def predict_intent(user_input):
    input_vector =
vectorizer.transform([user_input
])
    prediction =
model.predict(input_vector)
    return
intents[prediction[0]]

print(predict_intent("hello"))
```

```
print(predict_intent("what's the
weather like?"))
```

Using RNNs and Transformers for Natural Conversation

1. **Recurrent Neural Networks (RNNs)**:
   - o **RNNs** are designed for sequential data and are commonly used in chatbots to handle conversations. RNNs are capable of maintaining context across multiple turns in a conversation, making them suitable for dialogue systems.
   - o **Problem with Vanilla RNNs**: Standard RNNs struggle with long-term dependencies due to the **vanishing gradient problem**, making them less effective for complex conversations.
   - o **Solution**: **LSTM (Long Short-Term Memory)** and **GRU (Gated Recurrent Unit)** are variations of RNNs that help retain long-term context and are commonly used in NLP tasks like chatbots.
2. **Transformers**:
   - o The **Transformer** architecture, introduced in the paper "Attention is All You Need," has revolutionized NLP. Unlike RNNs, transformers do not rely on sequential data processing and instead use an attention mechanism to process all words in the input at once.
   - o **BERT, GPT-3**, and **T5** are examples of transformer-based models that are widely used for creating conversational agents.

These models can generate more fluent and natural conversations by learning from vast amounts of text data.

Example of a Transformer-based model (using Hugging Face's **Transformers** library for a pre-trained chatbot):

```python

from transformers import pipeline

# Load a pre-trained conversational model
chatbot = pipeline("conversational", model="microsoft/DialoGPT-medium")

# Generate a response
conversation = chatbot("Hello, how are you?")
print(conversation)
```

Transformers are particularly useful for **open-domain conversations** (where the chatbot is expected to handle a wide variety of topics), as they can generate responses that feel more natural and coherent over multiple exchanges.

Real-World Example: Building a Basic Chatbot for Customer Service

Let's build a simple chatbot that helps with customer service, providing answers to common queries like checking account balance, reporting an issue, and more.

1. **Define the Dataset and Intents**:
    o First, we define the intents that the chatbot will handle, such as checking the balance, reporting issues, and greeting users.

Example intents:

json

```
{
    "intents": [
        {"intent":        "greet",
"patterns":     ["hi",     "hello",
"hey"], "response": "Hello! How
can I help you today?"},
        {"intent":
"check_balance",       "patterns":
["What is my balance?", "Check my
balance",   "Account   balance"],
"response": "Your account balance
is $500."},
        {"intent":
"report_issue", "patterns": ["I
have   an   issue",   "Report   an
issue", "Help with my problem"],
```

```
"response": "Please describe the
issue, and I'll assist you."},
        {"intent":    "goodbye",
"patterns":    ["bye",    "goodbye",
"see you"], "response": "Goodbye!
Have a great day!"}
    ]
}
```

2. **Preprocess the Data**:
   o Tokenize the text and convert it into a format suitable for machine learning.

```python
from
sklearn.feature_extraction.text
import CountVectorizer
from sklearn.naive_bayes import
MultinomialNB
import json

# Define intents (in practice,
these would be loaded from a JSON
or database)
intents = {
    "greet":    ["hi",    "hello",
"hey"],
    "check_balance": ["What is my
balance?",  "Check  my  balance",
"Account balance"],
    "report_issue": ["I have an
issue", "Report an issue", "Help
with my problem"],
```

```
    "goodbye":            ["bye",
"goodbye", "see you"]
}

responses = {
    "greet": "Hello! How can I
help you today?",
    "check_balance":        "Your
account balance is $500.",
    "report_issue":       "Please
describe the issue, and I'll
assist you.",
    "goodbye": "Goodbye! Have a
great day!"
}

# Flatten the patterns into a
list and label them with
corresponding intents
patterns = [pattern for intent in
intents.values() for pattern in
intent]
labels = [label for label, intent
in intents.items() for _ in
intent]

# Vectorize the patterns
vectorizer = CountVectorizer()
X                             =
vectorizer.fit_transform(pattern
s)

# Train a Naive Bayes classifier
```

```
model = MultinomialNB()
model.fit(X, labels)
```

3. Define a Chatbot Function:

The chatbot will predict the intent of the user's input and provide the appropriate response.

```python
python

def chatbot_response(user_input):
    input_vector             =
vectorizer.transform([user_input])
    predicted_label          =
model.predict(input_vector)[0]
        return responses[predicted_label]

# Test the chatbot
print(chatbot_response("hi"))        #
Response: Hello! How can I help you
today?
print(chatbot_response("What is  my
balance?"))  # Response: Your account
balance is $500.
```

4. Refining the Chatbot:
   o As the chatbot is used, you can add more intents, responses, and improve the training data. You can also move from rule-based models to more advanced models, such as **RNNs** or **transformers**, to handle more complex conversations.

Summary

In this chapter, we explored the basics of **AI chatbots**, highlighting the difference between rule-based and machine learning-based chatbots. We discussed how chatbots work, from **user input** to **response generation**, and how **Recurrent Neural Networks (RNNs)** and **transformers** are used for more natural and flexible conversations.

We also walked through building a simple **customer service chatbot** using basic NLP techniques and machine learning models like **Naive Bayes**.

CHAPTER SUMMARY:

- AI chatbots simulate human conversation and can be used for a variety of tasks, from customer service to virtual assistants.
- **Rule-based chatbots** follow predefined patterns and rules, while **machine learning-based chatbots** learn from data and are more flexible.
- **RNNs** and **transformers** are advanced models that improve the chatbot's ability to handle complex and natural conversations.

CHAPTER 20

Deploying Machine Learning Models

Introduction to Deployment: From Prototype to Production

Once a machine learning model has been trained and evaluated, the next step is **deployment**, where the model is integrated into a live system and used to make predictions on real-world data. Deployment moves the model from the **development environment** (where it was built) to a **production environment** (where it can be accessed by users or applications).

Key Stages in Deployment:

1. **Model Development**: This involves training and evaluating the machine learning model on a local machine or development environment.
2. **Model Packaging**: Once the model is ready, it must be packaged into a format that can be used in production. This typically involves serializing the model (e.g., using **Pickle** or **Joblib**) so it can be loaded by a production system.
3. **Model Deployment**: The packaged model is then deployed as an API or integrated into a software system, allowing users or other systems to make predictions via web requests.
4. **Model Monitoring and Maintenance**: Once deployed, the model should be monitored for performance and accuracy. As data changes over

time, the model may need to be retrained or fine-tuned.

Why Deployment Matters:

- **Real-time Predictions**: Machine learning models need to be deployed in a way that allows them to make real-time or batch predictions in production.
- **Scalability**: Deployment ensures that the model can handle multiple requests or large datasets without performance degradation.
- **Operationalization**: Making a model accessible to users, businesses, or other systems, transforming it from a research project into a valuable tool.

Using Flask or FastAPI to Deploy Models as APIs

A common way to deploy machine learning models is by creating an API (Application Programming Interface) that allows external systems (like web applications or mobile apps) to interact with the model and request predictions.

1. **Flask**:
    - **Flask** is a lightweight Python web framework that is easy to use and suitable for deploying machine learning models as APIs.
    - Flask allows you to expose your model via HTTP endpoints, so users can send

requests and receive predictions in real-time.

Example of deploying a model with Flask:

```python

from flask import Flask, request, jsonify
import pickle
import numpy as np

# Load the trained model
model                      =
pickle.load(open('sentiment_mode
l.pkl', 'rb'))

# Initialize Flask app
app = Flask(__name__)

@app.route('/predict',
methods=['POST'])
def predict():
    # Get input data from the
request
    data                   =
request.get_json(force=True)
    text = data['text']

    # Preprocess the text and
make prediction
    prediction             =
model.predict([text])[0]
```

```
    # Return the prediction as a
JSON response
    return jsonify({'sentiment':
prediction})

if __name__ == '__main__':
    app.run(debug=True)
```

Steps:

- o **Load the model**: We load the serialized model (using **pickle** in this case).
- o **Create an endpoint**: We create a POST endpoint (`/predict`) that accepts JSON input.
- o **Preprocessing and prediction**: The model predicts the sentiment based on the input text, and the result is returned as a JSON response.

Once the Flask app is running, you can send a POST request to the `/predict` endpoint with some text and get the sentiment prediction.

2. **FastAPI**:
   - o **FastAPI** is another Python web framework that is faster and more modern than Flask, with built-in support for asynchronous APIs and automatic generation of OpenAPI documentation.
   - o FastAPI is particularly useful when you need high performance and want to

handle more complex requests asynchronously.

Example of deploying a model with FastAPI:

```python
from fastapi import FastAPI
from pydantic import BaseModel
import pickle
import numpy as np

# Load the trained model
model                   =
pickle.load(open('sentiment_mode
l.pkl', 'rb'))

# Initialize FastAPI app
app = FastAPI()

class InputText(BaseModel):
    text: str

@app.post("/predict")
async def predict(input_text:
InputText):
    # Preprocess the text and
make prediction
    prediction              =
model.predict([input_text.text])
[0]
    return           {"sentiment":
prediction}
```

```
if __name__ == '__main__':
    import uvicorn
    uvicorn.run(app,
host="0.0.0.0", port=8000)
```

Steps:

- o **Create a Pydantic model**: This is used for validating the input data (in this case, the text).
- o **Define an endpoint**: The `/predict` endpoint accepts POST requests and returns the sentiment prediction.
- o **Run the app**: You can run the FastAPI app with **uvicorn** to handle requests asynchronously.

FastAPI provides advantages such as automatic API documentation and validation, making it easier to deploy and test APIs.

Best Practices for Model Deployment

1. **Versioning**:
   - o It's important to version your models and APIs to track changes over time and ensure backward compatibility. For example, use versioning in your API endpoints (e.g., `/api/v1/predict`).
2. **Monitoring and Logging**:
   - o Set up **monitoring** to track the performance of the model in production (e.g., accuracy, response time). This can

be done using tools like **Prometheus** and **Grafana**.

- o **Logging** is crucial for debugging and understanding how the model is performing in real-time. Use structured logging to capture important details like input data, predictions, and errors.

3. **Scalability**:
   - o Ensure your model can handle an increase in requests. You can deploy your model on cloud platforms like **AWS**, **Google Cloud**, or **Azure**, which offer scalable solutions for deploying machine learning models.
   - o Consider using **containerization** tools like **Docker** to package your model and make it portable across different environments.

4. **Security**:
   - o Protect your API with **authentication** and **authorization** mechanisms to prevent unauthorized access. Use methods like **OAuth** or **API keys**.
   - o Ensure that sensitive data, such as customer information, is securely handled by the model and API.

5. **Automation**:
   - o **Automate the deployment pipeline** using CI/CD tools (e.g., **Jenkins**, **GitHub Actions**) to streamline updates and model retraining.

Real-World Example: Deploying a Sentiment Analysis
Model on a Website

Let's walk through deploying a **sentiment analysis model** on a website. We will use a pre-trained model for sentiment analysis (e.g., using a Naive Bayes classifier) and deploy it via a Flask or FastAPI-based API.

1. **Step 1: Prepare the Model**:
   - Train a sentiment analysis model using a dataset like **movie reviews** or **customer feedback**.
   - Serialize the model using **Pickle** or **Joblib**:

python

```python
import pickle
from sklearn.feature_extraction.text import CountVectorizer
from sklearn.naive_bayes import MultinomialNB

# Train a simple sentiment analysis model
vectorizer = CountVectorizer()
X = vectorizer.fit_transform(["I love this product", "This is terrible", "Great service!", "I hate waiting"])
y = [1, 0, 1, 0]  # 1 = positive sentiment, 0 = negative sentiment
```

```
model = MultinomialNB()
model.fit(X, y)

# Save the model and vectorizer
pickle.dump(model,
open('sentiment_model.pkl',
'wb'))
pickle.dump(vectorizer,
open('vectorizer.pkl', 'wb'))
```

2. **Step 2: Create the API** (using Flask or FastAPI):
   - o Follow the earlier example to create a Flask or FastAPI app that loads the model and vectorizer, takes user input (text), and returns a sentiment prediction.
3. **Step 3: Deploy the API**:
   - o Deploy your Flask or FastAPI application using **Docker** for easier deployment. You can host the API on **Heroku**, **AWS**, or any other cloud service.
   - o Example of running the Flask app with Docker:
     1. **Dockerfile**:

```
Dockerfile

FROM python:3.8-slim

WORKDIR /app

. /app
```

```
RUN    pip    install    -r
requirements.txt

CMD ["python", "app.py"]
```

2. Build and Run Docker Container:

```bash
docker build -t sentiment-
api .
docker run -p 5000:5000
sentiment-api
```

4. Step 4: Connect to a Front-End Web Application:

- On your website, you can create a simple form to allow users to input text. The form will send the input to the Flask or FastAPI API and display the predicted sentiment (positive or negative).
- Use JavaScript (AJAX) to send a POST request to the API and receive the response:

```javascript
async function sendText() {
    const      text      =
document.getElementById('user-
input').value;
```

```
        const    response    =    await
fetch('http://localhost:5000/pre
dict', {
        method: 'POST',
        headers: {
            'Content-Type':
'application/json'
        },
        body:    JSON.stringify({
text: text })
    });
    const    data    =    await
response.json();

document.getElementById('result'
).innerText    =    `Sentiment:
${data.sentiment}`;
}
```

Summary

In this chapter, we learned about the **deployment** process for machine learning models, from developing a model prototype to deploying it in production. We discussed how to deploy machine learning models as APIs using **Flask** or **FastAPI**, and how to apply best practices like **monitoring**, **scalability**, and **security**.

We also walked through a **real-world example** of deploying a **sentiment analysis model** on a website, where users can input text, and the model responds with sentiment predictions.

CHAPTER SUMMARY:

- **Model deployment** is essential for operationalizing machine learning models and making them accessible to real-world applications.
- **Flask** and **FastAPI** are popular Python web frameworks for deploying machine learning models as APIs.
- **Best practices** for deployment include versioning, monitoring, security, and automation to ensure robust and scalable solutions.

CHAPTER 21

Introduction to Cloud-Based AI with AWS, GCP, or Azure

What is Cloud Computing and Why is it Useful for AI?

Cloud computing refers to the delivery of computing services over the internet, allowing users to access and use computing resources like storage, computing power, and software applications without owning or maintaining the physical infrastructure. Instead, cloud providers offer these resources on-demand, typically via a subscription-based model.

Why Cloud Computing is Useful for AI:

1. **Scalability**: Cloud platforms allow users to scale resources up or down based on demand. This is especially useful for training machine learning models, which can require significant computational power.
2. **Cost-Efficiency**: Instead of investing in expensive hardware, users can rent computing resources (e.g., GPUs, TPUs) on an as-needed basis, paying only for what they use.
3. **Access to Advanced Tools**: Cloud platforms provide easy access to powerful AI and machine learning tools (e.g., pre-built models, deep learning frameworks, data storage, and orchestration services) that may be difficult or expensive to set up on local systems.

4. **Collaboration and Flexibility**: Cloud environments allow teams to collaborate easily, share resources, and run experiments remotely without needing powerful local machines.

5. **Integration with Big Data**: AI models often need large datasets for training. Cloud platforms provide seamless integration with big data tools and storage services (e.g., AWS S3, GCP BigQuery) to process and store massive datasets.

Introduction to Popular Cloud Platforms for AI

There are several major cloud platforms that offer AI and machine learning services, with each providing specialized tools, frameworks, and infrastructure to accelerate AI development.

1. **Amazon Web Services (AWS)**:
   - **AWS** is a comprehensive cloud platform that offers a wide range of services for AI, machine learning, and deep learning, including compute, storage, and specialized AI tools.
   - Popular AWS AI/ML services:
     - **SageMaker**: A fully managed service for building, training, and deploying machine learning models.
     - **Lambda**: Serverless computing that runs code without provisioning servers.

- **EC2 Instances**: Virtual machines that can be configured with powerful GPUs for deep learning.
- **Deep Learning AMIs**: Pre-configured Amazon Machine Images for deep learning, which include popular frameworks like TensorFlow, PyTorch, and MXNet.

2. **Google Cloud Platform (GCP)**:
   o **GCP** is Google's cloud offering, providing powerful machine learning tools, especially for deep learning and AI development.
   o Popular GCP AI/ML services:
     - **AI Platform**: A fully managed service for training and deploying machine learning models.
     - **TensorFlow on GCP**: TensorFlow, Google's deep learning framework, is deeply integrated with GCP for seamless model development and deployment.
     - **Google BigQuery**: A fully managed data warehouse for processing large datasets, often used in conjunction with machine learning models.

3. **Microsoft Azure**:
   o **Azure** is Microsoft's cloud platform, offering machine learning services and

tools tailored for enterprise AI development.

- o Popular Azure AI/ML services:
  - **Azure Machine Learning**: A comprehensive service for building, training, and deploying models with various tools and frameworks.
  - **Azure Cognitive Services**: Pre-built AI APIs for tasks like computer vision, speech recognition, and language understanding.
  - **Azure Databricks**: A collaborative platform for big data processing and machine learning based on Apache Spark.

Training Large Models in the Cloud

Training large models, especially deep learning models, requires significant computational resources (e.g., GPUs or TPUs) that may not be available on local machines. Cloud platforms provide access to these powerful resources on demand, enabling you to train large models efficiently.

1. **GPUs and TPUs for Training**:
   - o **GPUs (Graphics Processing Units)**: GPUs are specialized hardware designed for parallel processing, making them ideal for the matrix operations involved in deep learning.

- o **TPUs (Tensor Processing Units)**: TPUs are Google's custom-built hardware accelerators designed specifically for deep learning tasks. They provide even higher performance than GPUs for certain types of deep learning models, especially when using TensorFlow.

2. **Distributed Training**:
   - o Cloud platforms allow you to train models in parallel across multiple machines, effectively distributing the workload and speeding up training times.
   - o Services like **AWS SageMaker** or **Google AI Platform** provide managed environments for distributed training using multiple GPUs or TPUs.

3. **Auto-scaling and On-Demand Resources**:
   - o Cloud platforms allow you to automatically scale your resources based on demand. For example, AWS EC2 instances can be configured to automatically scale up to more powerful machines as needed, and then scale back down after the job is completed, making the process cost-efficient.

4. **Storage and Data Management**:
   - o AI model training often requires large datasets that need to be stored, processed, and accessed efficiently. Cloud platforms offer robust storage solutions (e.g., **AWS S3**, **Google Cloud Storage**) and data processing tools to handle massive datasets.

Real-World Example: Using AWS for Training a Deep Learning Model

Let's walk through how you can train a **deep learning model** (e.g., an image classification model) using **AWS**.

Step 1: Set Up an AWS EC2 Instance with GPU

1. **Create an EC2 Instance**:
   - Go to the AWS Management Console, select **EC2**, and launch a new instance.
   - Choose an instance type that has a GPU, such as **p2.xlarge** (which provides access to NVIDIA K80 GPUs) or **p3.xlarge** (with NVIDIA V100 GPUs for faster training).
2. **Install Dependencies**:
   - After launching the instance, SSH into the instance and set up the environment for deep learning.
   - Install **TensorFlow** or **PyTorch** using pip, as well as any other required dependencies:

```bash
pip install tensorflow
pip install keras
pip install numpy matplotlib
```

Step 2: Prepare the Data

For an image classification task, we can use a dataset like **CIFAR-10** or **ImageNet**. For simplicity, let's use **CIFAR-10**, which contains 60,000 32x32 color images in 10 classes.

python

```
from tensorflow.keras.datasets import
cifar10
import numpy as np

# Load CIFAR-10 dataset
(x_train, y_train), (x_test, y_test)
= cifar10.load_data()

# Normalize the images to have values
between 0 and 1
x_train, x_test = x_train / 255.0,
x_test / 255.0
```

Step 3: Build the Model

Let's define a simple **Convolutional Neural Network (CNN)** for image classification.

python

```
from tensorflow.keras import layers,
models

# Build a simple CNN model
model = models.Sequential([
```

219

```
    layers.Conv2D(32,        (3,       3),
activation='relu',    input_shape=(32,
32, 3)),
    layers.MaxPooling2D((2, 2)),
    layers.Conv2D(64,        (3,       3),
activation='relu'),
    layers.MaxPooling2D((2, 2)),
    layers.Conv2D(64,        (3,       3),
activation='relu'),
    layers.Flatten(),
    layers.Dense(64,
activation='relu'),
    layers.Dense(10,
activation='softmax')
])

# Compile the model
model.compile(optimizer='adam',
loss='sparse_categorical_crossentrop
y', metrics=['accuracy'])
```

Step 4: Train the Model on AWS EC2

Now, we can train the model using the **GPU-enabled EC2 instance**.

```
python
```

```
# Train the model using GPU
acceleration
model.fit(x_train,            y_train,
epochs=10,             batch_size=64,
validation_data=(x_test, y_test))
```

Step 5: Monitor the Training Process

While training the model on AWS, you can monitor the progress via **CloudWatch**, AWS's monitoring tool, or set up logging to track accuracy and loss metrics.

Step 6: Save the Model

Once training is complete, you can save the model to **S3** or download it to your local machine for future use.

```python
# Save the model to S3 or locally
model.save('cifar10_model.h5')
```

Step 7: Deploy the Model (Optional)

After training, you can deploy the model using **AWS SageMaker** or host it on an **EC2 instance** with a Flask API to make predictions in real time.

Summary

In this chapter, we explored **cloud computing** and its role in enabling scalable and efficient AI and machine learning workflows. We discussed how **AWS**, **GCP**, and **Azure** provide powerful tools and infrastructure for training large machine learning models, and how cloud services support advanced machine learning tasks like distributed training and model deployment.

We also walked through a **real-world example** of training a **deep learning model** on AWS using an **EC2 instance** with GPU acceleration.

CHAPTER SUMMARY:

- **Cloud computing** provides scalable, cost-efficient resources for training and deploying machine learning models.
- Platforms like **AWS**, **GCP**, and **Azure** offer specialized services for AI, including GPU/TPU instances, model training, and deployment tools.
- **AWS EC2** is a great choice for running deep learning models, and **SageMaker** can be used for more managed machine learning workflows.

CHAPTER 22

Working with Pre-trained Models

What Are Pre-trained Models and Why Should You Use Them?

Pre-trained models are machine learning models that have already been trained on large datasets, typically on tasks like image classification, language understanding, or object detection. These models are often built by researchers or organizations with access to vast amounts of data and computational resources, making it impractical for individual developers or small teams to train these models from scratch.

Why Use Pre-trained Models?

1. **Time and Cost Efficiency**: Training a deep learning model from scratch requires vast amounts of data, computational resources, and time. Pre-trained models save time and cost by leveraging existing knowledge learned from large datasets.
2. **Better Performance**: Pre-trained models often outperform models trained from scratch on smaller datasets. They have learned useful features from massive datasets (like ImageNet for images or large text corpora for NLP), which can be useful for similar tasks.
3. **Reduced Data Requirements**: Using pre-trained models can drastically reduce the amount of data required to train your model. Fine-tuning

a pre-trained model on your specific task often requires fewer data points than training a model from scratch.

4. **Transfer Learning**: Pre-trained models can be adapted to different tasks through a technique called **transfer learning**, where the knowledge gained from one domain (e.g., recognizing general objects in images) is transferred to a new but related task (e.g., classifying specific objects).

Using Transfer Learning to Fine-Tune Existing Models

Transfer learning is the process of taking a model that has been trained on one task (typically with a large dataset) and fine-tuning it to perform well on a different, but related, task. Instead of training a new model from scratch, transfer learning allows us to leverage pre-trained weights from models such as **VGG**, **ResNet**, or **BERT** for specific tasks like image classification or natural language processing.

Steps for Transfer Learning:

1. **Load a Pre-trained Model**: Load an existing model that has been trained on a large dataset (e.g., **ImageNet** for image classification).
2. **Freeze the Base Layers**: The early layers of pre-trained models capture general features (e.g., edges, textures for images), so you typically freeze these layers and only fine-tune the later layers.

3. **Fine-tune the Model**: Replace the final layers of the model with layers that match your specific task, and train the model on your dataset.

4. **Train the Model**: Train only the new layers while keeping the pre-trained layers frozen, or optionally, unfreeze some of the earlier layers for fine-tuning.

Advantages of Transfer Learning:

- **Less Training Data**: Transfer learning allows you to achieve good performance even with smaller datasets.
- **Faster Convergence**: Fine-tuning a pre-trained model requires fewer epochs to converge, making training faster.
- **Generalization**: The pre-trained model can generalize well to new data because it has learned high-level features from a large dataset.

Real-World Example: Using a Pre-trained Model for Image Classification

Let's walk through using a pre-trained model (e.g., **ResNet50**), which has been trained on **ImageNet** for image classification, and fine-tuning it for a new task—classifying specific objects (e.g., cats vs. dogs).

Step 1: Import Necessary Libraries and Load the Pre-trained Model

We'll use **Keras** with TensorFlow to load the pre-trained **ResNet50** model.

python

```
import tensorflow as tf
from    tensorflow.keras.applications
import ResNet50
from  tensorflow.keras.layers  import
Dense, GlobalAveragePooling2D
from  tensorflow.keras.models  import
Model
from
tensorflow.keras.preprocessing.image
import ImageDataGenerator
from      tensorflow.keras.optimizers
import Adam

# Load the pre-trained ResNet50 model,
excluding the top (fully connected)
layers
base_model                          =
ResNet50(weights='imagenet',
include_top=False, input_shape=(224,
224, 3))

# Freeze the base model (don't update
the weights during training)
base_model.trainable = False
```

Step 2: Add Custom Layers for Fine-Tuning

Next, we'll add a few custom layers on top of the pre-trained base model to match our specific task (binary classification: cats vs. dogs).

python

```python
# Add custom layers for the new
classification task
x = base_model.output
x = GlobalAveragePooling2D()(x)   #
Pool the output of the last
convolutional layer
x = Dense(1024, activation='relu')(x)
# Fully connected layer
predictions          =          Dense(1,
activation='sigmoid')(x)   # Output
layer for binary classification

# Create the final model
model                                   =
Model(inputs=base_model.input,
outputs=predictions)
```

Step 3: Prepare the Data for Training

We'll use **ImageDataGenerator** to load and preprocess the images for training and validation. This will handle image augmentation and normalization.

```python
python
```

```python
# Define data generators for loading
and augmenting the images
train_datagen                           =
ImageDataGenerator(rescale=1./255,
rotation_range=40,
width_shift_range=0.2,
```

```
height_shift_range=0.2,
shear_range=0.2, zoom_range=0.2,

horizontal_flip=True,
fill_mode='nearest')

validation_datagen                    =
ImageDataGenerator(rescale=1./255)

# Load the images from directories
(Assuming 'train' and 'validation'
directories are prepared)
train_generator                       =
train_datagen.flow_from_directory('t
rain/', target_size=(224, 224),

batch_size=32, class_mode='binary')

validation_generator                  =
validation_datagen.flow_from_directo
ry('validation/',  target_size=(224,
224),

batch_size=32, class_mode='binary')
```

Step 4: Compile the Model

We'll compile the model with a binary cross-entropy loss function since this is a binary classification task (cats vs. dogs).

```
python
```

```
# Compile the model
model.compile(optimizer=Adam(learnin
g_rate=0.0001),
loss='binary_crossentropy',
metrics=['accuracy'])
```

Step 5: Train the Model

We'll train the model for a few epochs, keeping the base model frozen.

```
python
```

```
# Train the model
history = model.fit(train_generator,
epochs=10,
validation_data=validation_generator
)
```

Step 6: Fine-Tune the Model (Optional)

After training the new layers, we can **unfreeze** some layers of the pre-trained base model and continue training for better fine-tuning.

```
python
```

```
# Unfreeze the last few layers of the
base model for fine-tuning
base_model.trainable = True
for layer in base_model.layers[:140]:
    layer.trainable = False
```

```python
# Re-compile the model (since we
unfreezed some layers)
model.compile(optimizer=Adam(learnin
g_rate=0.00001),
loss='binary_crossentropy',
metrics=['accuracy'])

# Continue training
history_fine_tuned                    =
model.fit(train_generator, epochs=10,
validation_data=validation_generator
)
```

Step 7: Evaluate and Use the Model

Finally, we can evaluate the model's performance on a test set and use it to make predictions on new images.

```
python
```

```python
# Evaluate the model on test data
test_generator                        =
validation_datagen.flow_from_directo
ry('test/', target_size=(224, 224),
batch_size=32, class_mode='binary')
loss,           accuracy             =
model.evaluate(test_generator)
print(f"Test accuracy: {accuracy *
100:.2f}%")

# Make predictions on new images
from    tensorflow.keras.preprocessing
import image
import numpy as np
```

```
# Load and preprocess a new image
img_path = 'new_image.jpg'
img       =      image.load_img(img_path,
target_size=(224, 224))
img_array = image.img_to_array(img)
img_array = np.expand_dims(img_array,
axis=0) / 255.0  # Normalize

# Predict the class (0 for cats, 1 for
dogs)
prediction = model.predict(img_array)
print("Prediction  (0  =  cat,  1  =
dog):", prediction)
```

Summary

In this chapter, we explored the concept of **pre-trained models** and how **transfer learning** can be used to fine-tune a model for a specific task. By leveraging pre-trained models like **ResNet50**, we were able to quickly adapt the model for a new image classification task (cats vs. dogs) without needing to train from scratch.

CHAPTER SUMMARY:

- **Pre-trained models** save time and computational resources by leveraging the knowledge learned from large datasets like ImageNet.

- **Transfer learning** allows you to adapt pre-trained models for specific tasks with minimal data and training time.
- **Fine-tuning** a model involves adding custom layers and adjusting the model's weights to perform well on a new task.

CHAPTER 23

Ethics in AI and Machine Learning

Introduction to Ethical Considerations in AI

As artificial intelligence (AI) and machine learning (ML) systems become increasingly integrated into various aspects of society, the ethical implications of these technologies are a growing concern. AI systems have the potential to transform industries, improve efficiency, and solve complex problems, but they also raise important ethical questions related to fairness, accountability, privacy, and transparency.

Why Ethical Considerations Matter:

- **Impact on Society**: AI can influence decision-making in critical areas such as healthcare, criminal justice, finance, and hiring, making it essential to ensure that these systems are fair and just.
- **Trust and Acceptance**: Public trust in AI is crucial for its widespread adoption. Ethical AI practices foster transparency and fairness, which builds confidence among users and stakeholders.
- **Accountability**: As AI systems make decisions that affect people's lives, there must be mechanisms to ensure that these decisions are accountable, explainable, and based on unbiased data.

Ethical AI is not just about preventing harm but also about promoting fairness, respect for privacy, and ensuring that AI systems work for the benefit of everyone, especially vulnerable and marginalized groups.

Bias and Fairness in Machine Learning Models

One of the most pressing ethical concerns in AI and machine learning is **bias**. Bias in machine learning can manifest in several ways, and it can lead to unfair and discriminatory outcomes.

Types of Bias in AI:

1. **Data Bias:**
   - Bias can arise from the data used to train the model. If the data reflects historical prejudices or inequalities, the model may learn to replicate these biases.
   - Example: If a facial recognition system is trained on a dataset with predominantly light-skinned individuals, it may perform poorly on individuals with darker skin tones.

2. **Label Bias:**
   - The labels used for supervised learning may be biased. If the labeling process involves subjective judgment or reflects societal biases, the model will learn from these biased labels.
   - Example: In a hiring model, if resumes are labeled with "successful" or

"unsuccessful" based on historical patterns, the system may reinforce existing gender or racial biases in hiring decisions.

3. **Algorithmic Bias**:
   o The model itself may introduce bias based on the algorithms used. Some algorithms may unintentionally favor certain groups or features, leading to unfair outcomes.
   o Example: A credit scoring model might overemphasize factors such as zip codes or credit history, which could disproportionately impact certain demographics.

Fairness in Machine Learning: Fairness in machine learning refers to the goal of ensuring that AI systems make decisions that are equitable across different groups of people. There are several approaches to fairness:

1. **Demographic Parity**: Ensures that different groups are treated equally by the model (e.g., no group is disproportionately negatively affected).
2. **Equal Opportunity**: Ensures that different groups have equal chances of receiving positive outcomes (e.g., applying the same thresholds for loan approvals for all groups).
3. **Individual Fairness**: Ensures that similar individuals are treated similarly by the model, meaning that the model should not discriminate against individuals based on sensitive features like race or gender.

Measuring Bias and Fairness:

- **Fairness metrics**: There are several metrics used to assess fairness in AI models, such as **demographic parity difference**, **equal opportunity difference**, and **disparate impact**.
- **Bias detection tools**: Tools like **AI Fairness 360** (IBM), **Fairness Indicators** (Google), and **What-If Tool** (TensorFlow) can be used to detect and mitigate bias in machine learning models.

How to Build Ethical and Transparent AI Systems

Building ethical AI systems requires careful consideration of various factors, including fairness, transparency, accountability, and privacy. Here are some key principles for creating responsible AI:

1. **Transparency**:
   o AI systems should be transparent and explainable. Users should be able to understand how decisions are being made and have access to the reasoning behind model predictions.
   o Techniques for improving transparency include:
       ▪ **Explainable AI (XAI)**: Methods such as **LIME** (Local Interpretable Model-agnostic Explanations) and **SHAP** (Shapley Additive Explanations) can help explain black-box models.

- **Model Documentation**: Providing clear documentation on how the model was built, the data it was trained on, and the potential limitations.

2. **Accountability**:
   - Developers and organizations should be accountable for the actions of their AI systems. This includes monitoring models in production to ensure they are working as intended and correcting any issues that arise.
   - **Auditability**: AI systems should be subject to regular audits to assess their fairness, accuracy, and compliance with ethical guidelines.

3. **Privacy and Data Protection**:
   - AI models often require large amounts of personal data. It is essential to ensure that this data is collected, processed, and stored in compliance with data protection laws (e.g., GDPR, CCPA).
   - Techniques such as **differential privacy** and **federated learning** can be used to protect individuals' privacy while still enabling effective AI modeling.

4. **Bias Mitigation**:
   - **Data Preprocessing**: Removing biased data or re-sampling the data to ensure balanced representation across groups can help reduce bias.
   - **Algorithmic Fairness**: Adjusting the learning algorithm to enforce fairness

constraints can help prevent the model from learning biased patterns.

- o **Post-Processing**: Applying fairness constraints after the model has been trained, such as adjusting decision thresholds to ensure equal treatment of different groups.

5. **Incorporating Ethical Frameworks**:
   - o **Ethical Guidelines**: Organizations can adopt ethical guidelines that align with established standards, such as the **IEEE Ethically Aligned Design** or the **AI Ethics Guidelines by the European Commission**.
   - o **Stakeholder Involvement**: Involve diverse stakeholders (e.g., ethicists, community representatives) in the design, development, and deployment of AI systems to ensure broader perspectives are considered.

Real-World Example: Identifying Bias in a Credit Scoring Model

Let's consider a real-world example of identifying and addressing bias in a **credit scoring model**. Credit scoring models are used by financial institutions to assess an individual's creditworthiness based on factors like income, credit history, and debt.

1. **Identifying Bias**:
   - o Suppose a credit scoring model uses **zip code** as a feature, which might indirectly

correlate with race or socio-economic status. This could lead to biased predictions where individuals from certain zip codes (often minority communities) are unfairly penalized.

- To detect this bias, we can use fairness metrics such as **disparate impact** or **demographic parity** to assess whether the model disproportionately impacts certain groups.

2. **Mitigating Bias**:
- **Pre-processing**: We could remove zip code as a feature to avoid the risk of indirect bias.
- **Algorithmic Fairness**: Apply fairness constraints during model training to ensure that the model does not unfairly disadvantage certain groups.
- **Post-processing**: After the model is trained, adjust the decision thresholds so that the model's predictions are more equitable across different groups.

3. **Evaluating the Model**:
- Evaluate the model using fairness metrics:
  - **Demographic Parity Difference**: Ensures that different groups have equal access to credit.
  - **Equal Opportunity Difference**: Ensures that the model provides equal opportunity for credit to qualified individuals, regardless of their group.

Example code to evaluate fairness:

python

```
from fairness_metrics import
demographic_parity,
equal_opportunity

# Assuming model predictions and
actual labels are available
predictions =
model.predict(X_test)
true_labels = y_test

# Evaluate demographic parity
dp_diff =
demographic_parity(predictions,
true_labels,
sensitive_feature='zip_code')
print(f"Demographic         Parity
Difference: {dp_diff}")

# Evaluate equal opportunity
eo_diff =
equal_opportunity(predictions,
true_labels,
sensitive_feature='zip_code')
print(f"Equal         Opportunity
Difference: {eo_diff}")
```

4. **Final Steps**:
   o Once bias has been detected and mitigated, the model should be retrained,

and fairness should be continuously monitored in production.
- The results and the steps taken to ensure fairness should be documented and shared transparently with stakeholders.

Summary

In this chapter, we discussed the ethical considerations that must be taken into account when developing and deploying AI and machine learning models. We explored issues such as **bias**, **fairness**, and **accountability**, and we provided strategies for building ethical and transparent AI systems.

CHAPTER SUMMARY:

- **Bias** in AI models can lead to discriminatory and unfair outcomes, making it crucial to detect and mitigate bias during model development.
- **Transfer learning** and other techniques can help in building ethical AI by ensuring fairness, transparency, and accountability in the development process.
- **Real-world examples**, like identifying bias in a credit scoring model, highlight the importance of fairness metrics and model evaluation to ensure equitable outcomes for all stakeholders.

CHAPTER 24

Advancing with Transfer Learning

What is Transfer Learning and Why is It Important?

Transfer learning is a machine learning technique where a model trained on one task is reused for a different, but related, task. Instead of training a model from scratch, transfer learning allows you to leverage the knowledge learned by a pre-trained model on a large dataset (e.g., ImageNet for images or large text corpora for natural language) and apply it to a new task with relatively little data.

Why Transfer Learning is Important:

1. **Faster Training**: Training a model from scratch requires large amounts of data and computing power. Transfer learning allows you to start with a pre-trained model and fine-tune it for your task, dramatically reducing training time.
2. **Data Efficiency**: It allows models to generalize well even when the available dataset is small, by transferring knowledge learned from a large dataset.
3. **Improved Performance**: Pre-trained models often perform better on tasks that are similar to the original task they were trained on because they have learned generalizable features.
4. **Leverages Pre-trained Knowledge**: It allows the model to benefit from the knowledge already embedded in a pre-trained model, such as

detecting edges in images or understanding syntactic structures in text.

Techniques for Transferring Knowledge from One Domain to Another

Transfer learning can be applied in different ways depending on the similarity between the source and target tasks. Below are the common techniques for transferring knowledge:

1. **Fine-Tuning**:
   - Fine-tuning involves taking a pre-trained model and updating the weights of the model to adapt it to a new task. In the fine-tuning process, you typically freeze the early layers of the model (which learn general features) and only retrain the later layers for your specific task.
   - Fine-tuning is particularly effective when the source and target tasks are closely related (e.g., object recognition on two different sets of images).
2. **Feature Extraction**:
   - In feature extraction, the pre-trained model is used as a fixed feature extractor. The pre-trained layers are not updated, and the output of these layers is passed through new layers that are trained on the new task.
   - This is often used when you have limited data and want to retain the general

features learned by the pre-trained model while applying them to a new problem.

3. **Domain Adaptation**:
   o Domain adaptation is a specialized form of transfer learning in which the source and target domains have different distributions. It attempts to make the feature space in the source domain more similar to the target domain, thus making the model more applicable to the target domain.
   o Example: Adapting a model trained on daytime images to work well on nighttime images.

4. **Zero-shot Learning**:
   o Zero-shot learning allows the model to transfer its learning to tasks or domains it hasn't seen before, by leveraging semantic representations like word embeddings or contextual information.
   o Example: A language model that can generate responses or understand questions even when it hasn't seen specific phrases before.

Real-World Example: Fine-tuning a Pre-trained Neural Network for a New Task

In this example, we'll fine-tune a pre-trained **ResNet50** model (trained on ImageNet) to classify images of cats and dogs. We will leverage transfer learning to adapt the model for this new classification task.

Step 1: Import Necessary Libraries and Load the Pre-trained Model

We'll use **Keras** with TensorFlow to load the pre-trained **ResNet50** model and fine-tune it for our new task.

python

```python
import tensorflow as tf
from tensorflow.keras.applications import ResNet50
from tensorflow.keras.layers import Dense, GlobalAveragePooling2D
from tensorflow.keras.models import Model
from tensorflow.keras.preprocessing.image import ImageDataGenerator
from tensorflow.keras.optimizers import Adam

# Load the pre-trained ResNet50 model, excluding the top (fully connected) layers
base_model = ResNet50(weights='imagenet', include_top=False, input_shape=(224, 224, 3))

# Freeze the base model (don't update the weights during training)
base_model.trainable = False
```

Step 2: Add Custom Layers for Fine-Tuning

We'll add new layers on top of the pre-trained model to perform our specific task—classifying images of cats and dogs.

python

```python
# Add custom layers for the new
classification task
x = base_model.output
x = GlobalAveragePooling2D()(x)   #
Pool the output of the last
convolutional layer
x = Dense(1024, activation='relu')(x)
# Fully connected layer
predictions         =         Dense(1,
activation='sigmoid')(x)   # Output
layer for binary classification

# Create the final model
model                              =
Model(inputs=base_model.input,
outputs=predictions)
```

Step 3: Prepare the Data for Training

We'll use **ImageDataGenerator** to preprocess and augment our images for training and validation.

python

```python
# Define data generators for loading
and augmenting the images
```

246

```python
train_datagen                        =
ImageDataGenerator(rescale=1./255,
rotation_range=40,
width_shift_range=0.2,

height_shift_range=0.2,
shear_range=0.2, zoom_range=0.2,

horizontal_flip=True,
fill_mode='nearest')

validation_datagen                   =
ImageDataGenerator(rescale=1./255)

# Load the images from directories
(Assuming 'train' and 'validation'
directories are prepared)
train_generator                      =
train_datagen.flow_from_directory('t
rain/', target_size=(224, 224),

batch_size=32, class_mode='binary')

validation_generator                 =
validation_datagen.flow_from_directo
ry('validation/',   target_size=(224,
224),

batch_size=32, class_mode='binary')
```

Step 4: Compile the Model

We'll compile the model with a binary cross-entropy loss function since this is a binary classification task (cats vs. dogs).

```python
python

# Compile the model
model.compile(optimizer=Adam(learnin
g_rate=0.0001),
loss='binary_crossentropy',
metrics=['accuracy'])
```

Step 5: Train the Model

Now, we can train the model for a few epochs, keeping the base model frozen.

```python
python

# Train the model
history = model.fit(train_generator,
epochs=10,
validation_data=validation_generator
)
```

Step 6: Fine-Tune the Model (Optional)

After training the new layers, we can **unfreeze** some layers of the pre-trained base model and continue training for better fine-tuning.

```python
python
```

248

```python
# Unfreeze the last few layers of the
base model for fine-tuning
base_model.trainable = True
for layer in base_model.layers[:140]:
    layer.trainable = False

# Re-compile the model (since we
unfreezed some layers)
model.compile(optimizer=Adam(learnin
g_rate=0.00001),
loss='binary_crossentropy',
metrics=['accuracy'])

# Continue training
history_fine_tuned                  =
model.fit(train_generator, epochs=10,
validation_data=validation_generator
)
```

Step 7: Evaluate and Use the Model

Finally, we can evaluate the model's performance on a test set and use it to make predictions on new images.

```
python
```

```python
# Evaluate the model on test data
test_generator                      =
validation_datagen.flow_from_directo
ry('test/', target_size=(224, 224),
batch_size=32, class_mode='binary')
loss,            accuracy           =
model.evaluate(test_generator)
```

```
print(f"Test accuracy: {accuracy *
100:.2f}%")

# Make predictions on new images
from tensorflow.keras.preprocessing
import image
import numpy as np

# Load and preprocess a new image
img_path = 'new_image.jpg'
img = image.load_img(img_path,
target_size=(224, 224))
img_array = image.img_to_array(img)
img_array = np.expand_dims(img_array,
axis=0) / 255.0  # Normalize

# Predict the class (0 for cats, 1 for
dogs)
prediction = model.predict(img_array)
print("Prediction (0 = cat, 1 =
dog):", prediction)
```

Summary

In this chapter, we explored **transfer learning** and its importance in machine learning, especially for tasks with limited data. We demonstrated how to **fine-tune a pre-trained neural network** (ResNet50) for a new task, such as classifying images of cats and dogs. We covered the steps of:

1. Loading a pre-trained model.

2. Adding custom layers for the new task.
3. Fine-tuning the model.
4. Evaluating the model's performance.

CHAPTER SUMMARY:

- **Transfer learning** enables you to leverage pre-trained models to improve performance on new tasks, saving time and computational resources.
- **Fine-tuning** involves adapting a pre-trained model to your specific task by adding new layers and adjusting the weights.
- Transfer learning is particularly useful when you have limited data but still want to achieve high-performance results.

CHAPTER 25

AI in Real-World Applications

Case Studies of AI in Healthcare, Finance, and Retail

AI has already started making significant impacts across various industries. Here are a few case studies of how AI is transforming healthcare, finance, and retail:

1. **AI in Healthcare**:
   - **Disease Diagnosis**: AI models are used to help diagnose diseases by analyzing medical images (e.g., **X-rays**, **CT scans**, and **MRI scans**). Machine learning algorithms, especially **convolutional neural networks (CNNs)**, can detect patterns in images that human doctors might miss.
     - **Example**: IBM's **Watson for Oncology** assists oncologists by analyzing medical literature, clinical trial data, and patient data to recommend personalized treatment plans.
   - **Drug Discovery**: AI models are used to accelerate the process of drug discovery by analyzing biological data and predicting which compounds may be effective treatments for certain diseases.
     - **Example**: **Atomwise** uses AI to predict the effectiveness of small

molecules in treating diseases like Ebola and cancer.

- o **Personalized Medicine**: AI can help customize treatment plans based on individual patient data, improving outcomes and reducing side effects. This can involve analyzing genetic data and patient history to recommend the most effective treatments.
  - **Example**: **DeepMind** has developed AI systems capable of predicting patient deterioration, providing early warnings for conditions like acute kidney injury.

2. **AI in Finance**:
   - o **Fraud Detection**: AI is widely used in fraud detection systems by analyzing transaction patterns and identifying unusual behavior that may indicate fraudulent activities. Machine learning algorithms can learn to recognize patterns of legitimate transactions and flag anything that deviates from that.
     - **Example**: **PayPal** uses machine learning to detect fraudulent transactions in real-time by analyzing billions of data points related to user behavior, transaction patterns, and device information.
   - o **Credit Scoring**: Machine learning models can help lenders assess the

creditworthiness of borrowers by analyzing a variety of factors, including social media activity, purchase history, and payment behaviors, in addition to traditional credit scores.

- **Example: Zest AI** uses machine learning to enhance credit scoring models, enabling more accurate assessments and expanding access to credit for individuals who may have been overlooked by traditional models.

o **Algorithmic Trading**: AI-powered algorithms can analyze massive amounts of financial data and execute trades at high speeds, capitalizing on market opportunities in real-time.

- **Example: Renaissance Technologies**, a hedge fund, uses AI and machine learning models for algorithmic trading, managing billions in assets with high-frequency trading strategies.

3. **AI in Retail**:

o **Customer Behavior Prediction**: AI is used to predict customer behavior by analyzing purchase history, browsing patterns, and other data. This allows retailers to personalize recommendations and improve customer engagement.

- **Example: Amazon** uses machine learning to recommend products based on previous purchases, items frequently bought together, and browsing history. The recommendations are dynamically adjusted based on real-time customer interactions.

- o **Inventory Management**: AI-powered systems can predict demand for products, optimizing inventory levels and reducing overstock or stockouts. By analyzing past sales data and market trends, AI can forecast future demand more accurately than traditional methods.
  - **Example**: **Walmart** uses AI and machine learning to optimize supply chain logistics and inventory management, helping ensure products are in stock at the right time and in the right place.
- o **Chatbots and Virtual Assistants**: Retailers use AI-powered chatbots and virtual assistants to provide customer service, answer product-related queries, and assist with order placement. These bots improve efficiency and customer satisfaction.
  - **Example**: **Sephora** employs a chatbot called **Sephora Virtual Artist** that uses AI to recommend makeup products based on customer preferences and virtual try-ons.

The Impact of AI on Industries and Society

AI is revolutionizing industries, improving efficiency, and changing how businesses interact with customers. However, its impact also raises important societal and ethical considerations.

1. **Economic Impact**:
   - **Job Displacement**: As AI systems automate routine tasks, certain jobs, particularly in manufacturing, retail, and data processing, may be displaced. However, AI also creates new job opportunities in fields like AI development, data science, and robotics.
   - **Productivity Gains**: AI has the potential to increase productivity across many sectors, from automating customer support in retail to accelerating drug discovery in healthcare. This can lead to lower costs and faster innovations.
2. **Societal Impact**:
   - **Improved Accessibility**: AI can improve accessibility for people with disabilities. For instance, AI-powered voice assistants like **Alexa**, **Siri**, and **Google Assistant** enable individuals with limited mobility to control their environment and access information hands-free.
   - **Personalization**: AI allows companies to personalize user experiences, from online shopping recommendations to personalized healthcare plans. This

enhances user satisfaction but can also raise concerns around privacy and data security.

- o **Ethical Concerns**: Issues such as bias in AI models, transparency in decision-making, and the ethical implications of AI-driven surveillance need to be addressed to ensure that AI benefits society as a whole.

3. **Regulation and Policy**:
   - o Governments and organizations are beginning to put frameworks in place to regulate AI use. The **European Union** has introduced the **AI Act**, which aims to establish clear rules for AI deployment, particularly for high-risk applications like healthcare and criminal justice.
   - o **AI Ethics**: With AI making decisions that affect people's lives, ethical considerations around fairness, accountability, and transparency are essential. Ensuring that AI systems are fair and non-discriminatory is a growing focus of the AI research community.

Real-World Example: Predicting Customer Behavior Using Machine Learning

Let's dive into a practical example of using machine learning to predict customer behavior, specifically for a retailer looking to predict whether a customer will make a purchase during a session on their website.

Step 1: Data Collection

We need data on customer interactions with the website, including features such as:

- **Session Duration**: How long the customer spent on the website.
- **Page Views**: The number of pages viewed during the session.
- **Referral Source**: Whether the customer came from an ad, social media, or direct search.
- **Previous Purchases**: Whether the customer has made purchases in the past.

Step 2: Preprocessing the Data

Before training the model, we preprocess the data:

- Handle missing values
- Normalize numerical features
- Encode categorical features

```python
import pandas as pd
from sklearn.preprocessing import StandardScaler, LabelEncoder

# Load the dataset
data = pd.read_csv('customer_behavior.csv')

# Fill missing values
```

```
data.fillna(method='ffill',
inplace=True)

# Normalize numerical features
scaler = StandardScaler()
data[['session_duration',
'page_views']]                      =
scaler.fit_transform(data[['session_
duration', 'page_views']])

# Encode categorical features
encoder = LabelEncoder()
data['referral_source']             =
encoder.fit_transform(data['referral
_source'])
```

Step 3: Model Selection and Training

We use a machine learning algorithm like **Logistic Regression** or **Random Forest** to predict whether a customer will make a purchase.

```
python

from sklearn.model_selection import
train_test_split
from      sklearn.ensemble      import
RandomForestClassifier
from      sklearn.metrics      import
accuracy_score, classification_report

# Define features (X) and target (y)
```

```
X = data[['session_duration',
'page_views', 'referral_source',
'previous_purchases']]
y = data['purchase_made']  # 1 =
purchase, 0 = no purchase

# Split the data into training and
test sets
X_train, X_test, y_train, y_test =
train_test_split(X, y, test_size=0.3,
random_state=42)

# Train a Random Forest model
model =
RandomForestClassifier(n_estimators=
100, random_state=42)
model.fit(X_train, y_train)

# Make predictions
y_pred = model.predict(X_test)

# Evaluate the model
accuracy = accuracy_score(y_test,
y_pred)
print(f"Accuracy: {accuracy *
100:.2f}%")
print(classification_report(y_test,
y_pred))
```

Step 4: Model Deployment

Once the model is trained, it can be deployed as a web service using a framework like **Flask** or **FastAPI**. The model can then be used to predict customer behavior in real-time as they interact with the website.

Summary

In this chapter, we explored the impact of **AI** across various industries like **healthcare**, **finance**, and **retail**, providing real-world examples of how AI is improving business operations and enhancing customer experiences. We also discussed the broader **impact of AI** on industries and society, highlighting economic changes, ethical considerations, and the importance of regulation.

We concluded with a practical example of **predicting customer behavior** using machine learning, demonstrating how AI can be applied to real-world challenges like forecasting purchases in retail.

CHAPTER SUMMARY:

- AI is transforming industries, offering both benefits and challenges in areas like **healthcare**, **finance**, and **retail**.
- The **societal impact** of AI includes improving accessibility, personalizing services, and addressing ethical concerns like fairness and transparency.
- **Machine learning** can be used to predict customer behavior, helping businesses make

data-driven decisions and enhance customer engagement.

CHAPTER 26

Challenges in AI and Machine Learning

Common Pitfalls in AI Projects

Building successful AI models involves more than just selecting the right algorithms. AI projects are complex and often come with a variety of challenges that can impact the model's performance and the overall project success. Below are some of the most common pitfalls in AI projects:

1. **Insufficient Data**:
   - **Problem**: Many machine learning models, especially deep learning models, require large amounts of labeled data to perform well. Without sufficient data, models are prone to overfitting or may fail to capture meaningful patterns.
   - **Solution**: Techniques like **transfer learning** or **data augmentation** can help when you have limited data. Additionally, using pre-trained models or semi-supervised learning can enable you to work with less labeled data.
2. **Bias in Data**:
   - **Problem**: Bias in data can result in models that reinforce existing stereotypes or make discriminatory predictions. This can lead to ethical concerns, particularly in sensitive areas like hiring, healthcare, or finance.

- **Solution**: Ensuring data diversity and using fairness metrics during model evaluation can help reduce bias. It's also important to continually monitor models to ensure that they do not inadvertently amplify biases.

3. **Scalability Issues**:
   - **Problem**: Machine learning models that work well on small datasets may not scale effectively to large datasets, especially when the volume of data increases or when the model must serve real-time predictions.
   - **Solution**: Implementing distributed training using cloud platforms (e.g., AWS, GCP) or adopting more scalable algorithms such as **random forests** or **XGBoost** can help address scalability. In addition, optimizing model inference (e.g., quantization, pruning) can reduce computation during prediction.

4. **Overfitting**:
   - **Problem**: Overfitting occurs when a model performs well on the training data but poorly on unseen data. This is often a result of the model being too complex or being trained for too many epochs.
   - **Solution**: Techniques like **cross-validation**, **early stopping**, and **regularization** (L1, L2) can help prevent overfitting and improve model generalization.

5. **Lack of Explainability**:

- o **Problem**: Many machine learning models, particularly **deep learning models**, are seen as "black boxes" because their internal decision-making processes are difficult to interpret. This lack of transparency can be a barrier to model adoption in regulated industries (e.g., healthcare, finance).
- o **Solution**: Implementing **explainable AI (XAI)** techniques, such as **LIME** or **SHAP**, can help provide insights into how a model makes decisions, increasing trust and accountability.

How to Deal with Insufficient Data, Bias, and Scalability Issues

1. **Dealing with Insufficient Data**:
   - o **Data Augmentation**: For image-based tasks, you can artificially increase the dataset size by applying transformations like rotations, flips, and scaling. This helps the model generalize better.
     - ▪ Example: If you have a small set of images for a classification task, you can create new images by rotating or flipping existing ones.
   - o **Synthetic Data Generation**: In cases where it's difficult to obtain real data, synthetic data generated by tools like **Generative Adversarial Networks (GANs)** can be useful, especially in

domains like healthcare (e.g., generating medical images).

- o **Transfer Learning**: Leverage models pre-trained on large datasets and fine-tune them for your specific task. This allows you to build high-performing models with fewer data points.
- o **Semi-supervised Learning**: Combine labeled and unlabeled data for training. This is particularly useful when labeling data is expensive or time-consuming.

2. **Dealing with Bias**:

- o **Bias Detection**: Use fairness metrics to evaluate your model for bias. These metrics include:
  - **Demographic Parity**: Ensuring that the model's decisions are independent of sensitive attributes like gender or race.
  - **Equal Opportunity**: Ensuring that the model provides equal true positive rates across different groups.
- o **Bias Mitigation**: Bias can be reduced by:
  - Ensuring diverse and representative datasets.
  - Re-sampling techniques (e.g., over-sampling underrepresented groups or under-sampling overrepresented groups).
  - Adapting model algorithms with fairness constraints during training.

- o **Regular Auditing**: Continuously audit the model's performance to ensure that bias does not creep back into the system over time.
3. **Dealing with Scalability Issues**:
   - o **Cloud-based Solutions**: Utilize cloud infrastructure like **AWS**, **Google Cloud**, or **Azure** to handle large datasets and perform distributed training. These platforms offer high-performance computing resources such as GPUs and TPUs for deep learning tasks.
   - o **Model Compression**: Use techniques like **pruning**, **quantization**, and **knowledge distillation** to reduce the size and complexity of your model, making it more efficient for deployment in real-time applications.
   - o **Distributed Training**: For large-scale problems, distributed training across multiple machines can accelerate model training. Frameworks like **TensorFlow** and **PyTorch** support distributed training, enabling you to scale your models across clusters.

Overcoming Challenges and Improving Models Over Time

Machine learning is an iterative process. After the initial deployment, models must be continuously monitored and improved over time to maintain their accuracy and relevance.

1. **Continuous Monitoring**:
   - Once your model is in production, monitor its performance using key metrics (e.g., accuracy, precision, recall) to ensure it continues to perform well as new data comes in.
   - Implement **model drift detection**, which monitors if the model's predictions start to degrade over time due to changes in the underlying data distribution.
2. **Retraining Models**:
   - As new data becomes available, periodically retrain your model to keep it up-to-date. You can use a process called **online learning**, where the model is updated incrementally as new data is received.
   - **Active learning** is another technique where the model queries a human to label the most uncertain or valuable data points, improving the model's performance with fewer labeled examples.
3. **Hyperparameter Tuning**:
   - Continuously fine-tune your model by experimenting with different hyperparameters using techniques like **grid search**, **random search**, or **Bayesian optimization** to improve model performance.
   - Automated machine learning (AutoML) platforms, such as **Google Cloud AutoML** or **H2O.ai**, can also help by automating the model selection,

hyperparameter tuning, and feature engineering processes.

4. **Cross-domain Collaboration**:
   o Encourage collaboration between data scientists, domain experts, and ethical review boards. This helps to ensure that the model is built with domain-specific knowledge, is fair, and addresses business objectives.

Real-World Example: Handling Noisy Data in Time-Series Forecasting

In time-series forecasting, noisy data is a common challenge. For example, predicting stock prices or demand for products can be affected by external factors (e.g., market shocks, seasonality) that introduce noise into the data.

Step 1: Data Preprocessing and Cleaning

First, we need to preprocess the time-series data to handle missing values and noise.

```python
import pandas as pd
import numpy as np

# Load the time-series data (e.g., stock prices)
data = pd.read_csv('stock_prices.csv',
```

```
parse_dates=['date'],
index_col='date')

# Handle missing values (forward fill
or interpolation)
data.fillna(method='ffill',
inplace=True)

# Apply smoothing (moving average) to
reduce noise
data['smoothed']                       =
data['price'].rolling(window=5).mean
()
```

Step 2: Dealing with Outliers

Outliers can significantly impact the performance of time-series models. We can detect and remove outliers using statistical methods.

```
python

# Detecting outliers using IQR
(Interquartile Range)
Q1 = data['price'].quantile(0.25)
Q3 = data['price'].quantile(0.75)
IQR = Q3 - Q1

# Define the upper and lower bounds
for detecting outliers
lower_bound = Q1 - 1.5 * IQR
upper_bound = Q3 + 1.5 * IQR

# Remove the outliers
```

```python
data    =    data[(data['price']    >=
lower_bound)   &   (data['price']   <=
upper_bound)]
```

Step 3: Model Training

After preprocessing the data, we can train a time-series forecasting model such as **ARIMA** or a **LSTM** (Long Short-Term Memory) network to predict future values.

```
python
```

```python
from        statsmodels.tsa.arima.model
import ARIMA

# Train an ARIMA model (a simple time-
series model)
model    =    ARIMA(data['smoothed'],
order=(5, 1, 0))   # (p, d, q) values
for ARIMA
model_fit = model.fit()

# Make predictions
forecast                          =
model_fit.forecast(steps=10)
print(f"Predicted           values:
{forecast}")
```

Step 4: Evaluating the Model

Evaluate the model using metrics like **Mean Squared Error (MSE)** or **Root Mean Squared Error (RMSE)**.

```
python
```

```
from       sklearn.metrics       import
mean_squared_error

# Calculate the RMSE between the
predicted and actual values
rmse                            =
np.sqrt(mean_squared_error(data['smo
othed'][-10:], forecast))
print(f"RMSE: {rmse}")
```

Step 5: Continuous Improvement

Monitor the performance of the model over time, and retrain it periodically with the most recent data. Use techniques like **model ensemble** or **hyperparameter tuning** to improve forecasting accuracy.

Summary

In this chapter, we discussed some of the common challenges in AI and machine learning projects, including issues related to **insufficient data**, **bias**, and **scalability**. We also explored ways to **overcome these challenges**, such as data augmentation, bias mitigation, and cloud-based solutions for scalability. Additionally, we highlighted the importance of **continuous model improvement** and monitoring to ensure that AI models perform effectively over time.

We also walked through a **real-world example** of handling **noisy data in time-series forecasting**, showcasing how to preprocess, clean, and train a model to predict future trends.

CHAPTER SUMMARY:

- AI projects often face challenges such as insufficient data, bias, and scalability issues that must be addressed for successful implementation.
- Techniques like **transfer learning**, **bias mitigation**, and **data augmentation** can help overcome these challenges.
- **Continuous monitoring**, **retraining**, and **model improvement** are essential to ensure that AI models remain accurate and effective.

CHAPTER 27

The Future of AI and Machine Learning

Emerging Trends in AI: Quantum Computing, Self-Driving Cars, and AI Ethics

As AI continues to evolve, several emerging trends and technologies are shaping the future of machine learning. These innovations are pushing the boundaries of what's possible and opening up new possibilities for industries and applications.

1. **Quantum Computing**:
    - **What is Quantum Computing?**: Quantum computing is a revolutionary field that leverages the principles of quantum mechanics to process information in ways that traditional classical computers cannot. Quantum computers use quantum bits (qubits) instead of traditional binary bits, allowing for the processing of complex problems exponentially faster than classical machines.
    - **Impact on AI and Machine Learning**: Quantum computing has the potential to accelerate machine learning by enabling faster computations, solving optimization problems, and simulating quantum systems that are impossible for classical computers to model. This could drastically reduce the time needed to train

deep learning models and handle large datasets.

- o **Emerging Quantum Machine Learning**: Quantum machine learning (QML) combines quantum computing with machine learning algorithms to process data more efficiently and solve complex problems, such as improving pattern recognition in large datasets or developing more sophisticated models in healthcare.

2. **Self-Driving Cars**:
  - o **AI in Autonomous Vehicles**: Self-driving cars rely on AI and machine learning to navigate roads, make real-time decisions, and interact with their environment. These vehicles use a combination of **computer vision**, **reinforcement learning**, **sensor fusion**, and **deep learning** to understand the surroundings and make safe driving decisions.
  - o **The Road to Fully Autonomous Cars**: While many companies, such as **Tesla**, **Waymo**, and **Uber**, have made strides in developing autonomous vehicles, challenges like real-time decision-making, safety, and regulatory concerns still need to be addressed. AI plays a central role in improving the performance of self-driving cars, particularly in **predicting the behavior of other**

vehicles and **navigating complex traffic scenarios**.

- o **Impact on Society**: The widespread adoption of autonomous vehicles could revolutionize transportation by reducing accidents, improving traffic efficiency, and transforming industries like logistics, public transportation, and ride-sharing.

3. **AI Ethics**:

- o **Ethical Challenges in AI**: As AI systems become more integrated into society, ethical concerns are increasingly in focus. Issues like **bias**, **transparency**, **accountability**, and **privacy** are crucial in ensuring that AI is used responsibly.

- o **AI Fairness**: Ensuring fairness in AI models is essential to prevent discrimination against certain groups based on race, gender, or socioeconomic status. This includes addressing **algorithmic bias** and making models more interpretable and accountable.

- o **AI for Social Good**: There is a growing focus on using AI to tackle societal challenges, such as **climate change**, **poverty**, and **global health**. Ethical AI practices can guide the development of AI systems that prioritize the welfare of humanity and minimize negative societal impacts.

What's Next for Machine Learning?

As machine learning continues to advance, here are some of the key developments to watch for in the coming years:

1. **AI-Driven Automation**:
   - **Workplace Automation**: AI is expected to drive further automation in the workplace, replacing routine and manual tasks across industries like manufacturing, finance, healthcare, and customer service. While this could lead to greater efficiency and productivity, it also brings concerns about job displacement and the need for reskilling workers.
   - **Collaborative AI**: In the future, machine learning models will not only automate tasks but also collaborate with humans in real-time, improving decision-making and augmenting human capabilities. For example, AI assistants could work alongside professionals in industries like medicine, law, and engineering, offering suggestions, analyzing data, and making predictions.
2. **Edge AI**:
   - **AI at the Edge**: Edge AI refers to the deployment of machine learning models on devices at the "edge" of a network, such as smartphones, wearables, and IoT (Internet of Things) devices. This allows for real-time data processing and

decision-making without the need to send data to centralized servers, reducing latency and bandwidth usage.

- o **Applications**: Edge AI can be applied in fields like **smart homes**, **healthcare**, **autonomous vehicles**, and **industrial automation**, where quick decision-making and reduced dependency on cloud infrastructure are crucial.

3. **Explainable AI (XAI)**:
   - o **The Need for Transparency**: One of the ongoing challenges in AI is the lack of transparency in how models make decisions. **Explainable AI (XAI)** is an emerging field aimed at making machine learning models more interpretable and understandable to humans. This is especially important in high-stakes fields like healthcare, finance, and criminal justice, where AI decisions can have significant impacts on people's lives.
   - o **Research into XAI**: Several approaches are being developed to create more transparent AI systems, such as **LIME** (Local Interpretable Model-agnostic Explanations) and **SHAP** (Shapley Additive Explanations), which help explain model predictions by providing insights into the features that drive decisions.

4. **General AI (AGI)**:
   - o **From Narrow AI to General AI**: Current AI systems are considered

"narrow" or "weak" AI, meaning they are designed to perform specific tasks (e.g., image recognition, language translation). However, researchers are working toward the development of **Artificial General Intelligence (AGI)**, which would have the ability to perform any cognitive task that a human can do.

- **Challenges and Concerns**: AGI could lead to advancements in creativity, problem-solving, and human-like reasoning. However, it also raises questions about control, safety, and the potential risks of autonomous systems surpassing human intelligence. Research is focused on ensuring AGI is developed in a safe and ethical manner.

Resources for Continued Learning and Staying Up-to-Date in AI

1. **Online Courses and Certifications**:
   - **Coursera** and **edX**: Platforms like Coursera and edX offer a wide range of AI and machine learning courses from top universities, including **Stanford** and **MIT**. Popular courses include Andrew Ng's **Machine Learning** course and **Deep Learning Specialization**.
   - **Udacity**: Offers a **Nanodegree program** in AI and machine learning, which includes hands-on projects and mentorship.

- o **Fast.ai**: An online resource for practical deep learning courses designed to be accessible to beginners and advanced learners.

2. **Books and Publications**:
   - o **Books**: **"Deep Learning"** by Ian Goodfellow, Yoshua Bengio, and Aaron Courville; **"Hands-On Machine Learning with Scikit-Learn, Keras, and TensorFlow"** by Aurélien Géron.
   - o **Research Papers**: Stay up-to-date by reading AI research papers published in top conferences such as **NeurIPS, ICML, CVPR**, and **ACL**.
   - o **Blogs and News Sites**: Websites like **Towards Data Science**, **ArXiv**, and **AI Weekly** provide articles and research updates on AI and machine learning.

3. **Communities and Forums**:
   - o **Stack Overflow**: Participate in AI and machine learning communities on Stack Overflow to get help with coding questions and learn from other developers.
   - o **GitHub**: Contribute to open-source AI projects, collaborate with the community, and explore repositories like **TensorFlow** and **PyTorch** for hands-on learning.
   - o **Reddit**: Subreddits like **r/MachineLearning** and **r/learnmachinelearning** provide discussions, resources, and news related to AI.

4. **Conferences and Events**:
   - Attending AI conferences such as **NeurIPS**, **ICML**, and **CVPR** can help you stay at the cutting edge of AI research and network with experts in the field. Many of these conferences are now held virtually, making them more accessible to global participants.

Your Next Steps After Finishing This Book: Building Your Own Projects

1. **Start Small**: Begin by applying what you've learned to small projects that interest you. For example, you can start with a basic machine learning model for a classification or regression task, and gradually work up to more complex projects involving deep learning and transfer learning.
2. **Work on Real-World Datasets**: Participate in online machine learning competitions like those on **Kaggle** or contribute to open-source AI projects on **GitHub**. Working with real-world datasets will give you a deeper understanding of the challenges that arise when building machine learning models.
3. **Focus on Specific Domains**: If you're particularly interested in a certain domain, like healthcare, finance, or autonomous vehicles, consider focusing on AI projects that address problems in those areas. For example, you can work on a healthcare dataset for predicting

patient outcomes or a finance dataset for predicting stock prices.

4. **Build a Portfolio**: Document your projects and create a portfolio of your work. Showcase your projects on platforms like **GitHub**, **LinkedIn**, or **Kaggle** to demonstrate your skills to potential employers or collaborators.

5. **Contribute to AI Research**: If you're inclined toward research, consider writing papers or collaborating on AI research projects. You can submit papers to conferences or journals, or collaborate with universities and research labs.

Summary

In this chapter, we explored the **future of AI and machine learning**, highlighting emerging trends such as **quantum computing**, **self-driving cars**, and the importance of **AI ethics**. We discussed the evolution of AI technologies and their potential to shape industries and society in profound ways.

We also provided **resources for continued learning** in AI and machine learning, including online courses, books, communities, and conferences, to help you stay up-to-date with the latest advancements.

Finally, we outlined **next steps** after finishing this book, encouraging you to build your own AI projects, contribute to open-source communities, and focus on specific areas of interest.

CHAPTER SUMMARY:

- AI is evolving rapidly, with emerging technologies like **quantum computing** and **self-driving cars** poised to transform industries.
- **AI ethics** remains a crucial aspect of AI development, ensuring that systems are fair, transparent, and accountable.
- Continuing your learning journey through **online resources**, **community engagement**, and **hands-on projects** will help you stay at the forefront of AI advancements.

www.ingramcontent.com/pod-product-compliance
Lightning Source LLC
LaVergne TN
LVHW022337060326
832902LV00022B/4091